MW00345136

Vegan Crock Pot Cookbook for Beginners

600-Day Ultra-Convenient, Super-Tasty Plant-Based Recipes for Smart People to Master Your Favorite Kitchen Device

Fenom Slytea

Table of contents

Chapter 7: Vegan Crock Pot Dessert Recipes...............124

Conclusion...144

Introduction

The Vegan Crock Pot Cookbook may provide a varied mix of flavors, rich aroma as per the characteristic preparation method of regional culinary practices, but they are sure to impress you with its unique tastes and flavors. That are not only difficult to resist but also leaves you wanting for more and take up a regular practice of cooking these culinary vegan crock pot recipes to savor these delights for your taste buds and healthy lifestyle.

You don't need to spend hours in the kitchen or buy expensive ingredients to create delicious, creative, plant-based meals. The Vegan Crock Pot Cookbook is dedicated to providing you with nutritious recipes for a healthy vegan diet.

Chapter 1: The Basics of Vegan

What is Veganism?

According to the Vegan Society, veganism refers to "a way of living that attempts to exclude all forms of animal exploitation and cruelty be it for food, clothing or any other purpose." In other words, the vegan diet is a plant-based diet and eliminates the consumption of eggs, dairy, and any product that comes from animals.

While dietary veganism is restricted to the non-consumption of animal products, other forms of veganism eliminates that use of animal products, such as silk, leather, fur, and wool.

Why Vegan?

People who decide to go vegan do so for several reasons, one of which is to stand against cruelty to animals. This is because modern farming practices often mean animals live in tight cages and pens under generally deplorable living conditions.

In addition, many vegans are against the killing of animals for the purpose of consuming the meat.

Another reason why many people switch to veganism is to protest the environmental impact bought about by raising livestock. Compared to the production of plant-based alternatives, animal agriculture requires the use of more resources and leaves a higher carbon footprint.

Better health is one other major factor why veganism has become more popular in recent years. Vegan diets have been linked to lower body mass index and lower body weight. A plant-based diet has also been associated with lower risk of heart disease, cancer, and cognitive impairment like Alzheimer's.

Benefits of Vegan Diet

Veganism may seem too restrictive for many, but proponents believe the benefits outweigh the challenges of having to find meat-free alternatives to meals that they were used to eating.

Benefit # 1 - Good overall health

A diet that eliminates animal products and animal fats improves overall health in the following ways:

- Non-consumption of animal fats, such as trans fats and saturated fats, which raise the level of LDL or bad cholesterol in the body leads to lower risk of heart disease and certain cancers.
- By avoiding the consumption of animal products, vegans avoid chemicals and environmental toxins that may be transferred to humans through animal fats.
- Because the vegan diet is naturally rich in fiber and focuses on the consumption of whole grains, it can help lower blood sugar levels.
- A plant-based diet that includes probiotics could also reduce arthritis pain as it can lessen inflammation and improve the body's ability to absorb nutrients.

Benefit # 2 - Improved physical fitness

When a balanced diet is followed, vegans are likely to be more physically fit than their meat-eating counterparts.

One of the reasons why is because the vegan diet is often packed with nutrients that support the recovery period of the muscles in between trainings. Because of their consumption of extra nutrients and elimination of saturated fats, vegans typically have better levels of endurance and enjoy more flexibility.

There is also lower tendency for injuries as the diet does not contain foods that weaken the tissues and bones.

Benefit # 3 – Better weight management

Animal products are higher in fats, which equates to higher calories. Because animal sources are eliminated from the diet, vegans are likely to be better at managing their weight. In other words, losing weight as well as keeping the weight off is easier on a plant-based diet.

Benefit # 4 – Enhanced mood

The vegan diet is composed of foods that are rich in nutrients, such as unsaturated fats, omega-3 fatty acids, complex carbohydrates, and magnesium. These nutrients are necessary for proper brain function, including mood regulation.

Studies also suggest that microbes found in the gut affect mood and consuming fiber and probiotics as well as limiting the intake of animal fats and products help ensure that there is a high level of good bacteria in the gut.

Guidelines and Rules for Eating Vegan

There are no hard and fast rules for eating vegan. However, whether consciously or unconsciously, vegans often follow these guidelines in their food choices:

- **Seasonality**

Seasonal fruits and vegetables aren't just cheaper, they are also more nutritious and delicious as they are at their peak. Consuming produce that are in season also offers the bonus of being more environment friendly as these products are often found locally.

- **Going for healthy fats**

Good fats are generally found in seeds and nuts. These fats are considered healthy because they help in the absorption of other nutrients, as well as in aiding hormone production and formation of cell membranes. Healthy fats also help regulate genetic function.

- **Boosting protein intake**

The body needs protein to create and repair tissues and produce hormones and enzymes. Protein also makes up the blood, skin, muscles, cartilage, and bones, which is why it is important for any diet to contain enough protein to keep a person in good health. The most common plant-based sources of protein are beans, legumes, nuts, spirulina, and soy products, such as tofu, edamame, and tempeh, which are major components of most vegan diets.

- **Loading up on fiber**

Compared to their meat-eating counterparts, vegans consume more whole grains, nuts, seeds, legumes, as well as vegetables and fruits. Thus, they get a fair share of fiber from their diet.

- **Supplementing**

Despite eating a balanced diet, nutrient deficiency is common among vegans. Vitamin B12, for example, is usually lacking in the vegan diet because it is mostly found in animal sources like beef, organ meats, sardines, clams, tuna, and trout. For this reason, vegans are advised to take vitamin B12 supplements or consume more fortified foods.

What to Eat

Today, there are plenty of vegan ingredient alternatives that it's not too difficult to whip up some of the meal's vegans were used to eating before going on a completely plant-based diet.

Apart from fruits and vegetables, a typical vegan diet consists of:

- Tofu
- Tempeh
- Seitan
- Beans
- Lentils
- Seeds
- Nuts and nut milks
- Molasses and maple/rice syrup
- Ready-made vegan products like vegan meat, vegan cheese, plant-based yogurt, and others

What Not to Eat

All foods that originate from animals or contain animal products are on the do-not-eat list, such as:

- Beef
- Pork
- Chicken
- Fish
- Seafood
- Dairy
- Eggs
- Honey
- Foods that contain ingredients of animal origin, such as some wine and beer and certain chewing gums

Tips for Success

If you're already following a vegetarian diet, making the switch to an exclusively plant-based diet is much easier and has a higher chance of success. Thus, if animal products are part of most of your meals, try going vegetarian first.

You can then gradually replace eggs, dairy, and fish with vegan alternatives so the shift will be more manageable and sustainable.

The following are examples of other tips to help you successfully follow the vegan diet:

- Stock up on vegan staples, such as tofu, nuts, seeds, and vegan condiments.
- Apart from eating a balanced meal, make sure that you are getting enough of all the vital nutrients by taking supplements or consuming fortified foods.
- Find a group of like-minded individuals who can offer support and meal prep ideas. If you can't find vegans in your circle of friends, try checking online for social media groups or meetups that you can join.
- Many restaurants cater to people with various dietary requirements so eating out shouldn't be too difficult. However, you can always call ahead or check the establishment's website to make sure they have vegan options.
- To maximize the health benefits, you get from having a plant-based diet, it's necessary that you make the necessary lifestyle changes, such as exercising, getting adequate sleep, and managing stress.
- It's important to talk to your doctor if you have a health condition that may become aggravated by a sudden change in diet.

Make meal planning and meal prep part of your routine.

Chapter 2: The Basics of Crock Pot

How Does a Crock Pot Work?

The crockpot is a kitchen appliance that is a type of a slow cooker.

A slow cooker is designed to create meals by slowly cooking the ingredients over either low or high heat.

It works by trapping the heat inside the device and cooking food for a much longer period. This brings out the flavor of the food, and simmers ingredients in their own juice for long hours. This creates rich and deep flavors that you can't get from grilling, frying and baking.

The Benefits of a Crock Pot

The crockpot is easy to use and economical. It saves you time, energy and even money.

It saves time and effort because it requires minimal active preparation on your part. You simply have to dump the ingredients in the crockpot, and set it to do its job. You can leave it and attend to other important tasks on hand.

It also helps save money because it allows you to make use of cheaper cuts of meat. Slow cooking cheaper cuts results in tender and succulent meat that you can't get by just frying or boiling.

Tips and Tricks for Using a Crock Pot

Here are some helpful tips and tricks for using your crockpot:

- Read the manual – Just like when you're using a new appliance for the first time, it's imperative that you first read the manual of your crockpot to ensure that you know how it works, and you know how to take good care of it. Most have two settings: low setting which cooks food between six and 10 hours, and high setting, which cooks food between four and six hours.
- Do not leave your home or sleep while cooking – While you can leave the crockpot to do its job of cooking your food, it is still not advisable to leave it alone in the house or to sleep and leave it on cooking overnight.
- Use liners to make cleaning easier – There are liners that you can use inside the crockpot so that it'll be easier and quicker for you to clean it up.
- Thaw frozen meat or poultry first before cooking – This quickens the cooking process

and ensures that the food is cooked evenly.

Do not overcrowd your crockpot – Make sure that you don't fill up your crockpot to the brim and to leave some space for heat to circulate.

Chapter 3: Vegan Crock Pot Breakfast Recipes

Apple Crumble

Preparation time: 10 minutes
Cooking time: 4 hours
Servings: 4

Ingredients:

- 1 cup granola
- 2 apples, peeled, cored and cut into chunks
- 1/8 cup maple syrup
- 2 tablespoons coconut butter
- 1/4 cup apple juice
- 1/2 teaspoon nutmeg, ground
- 1 teaspoon cinnamon, ground

Directions:

1. Put the apples in your crock pot.
2. Add maple syrup, butter, apple juice, nutmeg and cinnamon.
3. Stir gently, sprinkle granola on top, cover and cook on Low for 4 hours.
4. Divide into bowls and serve.

Enjoy!

Nutrition:

- Calories 160
- Fat 1
- Fiber 2
- Carbs 4
- Protein 5

Hearty French Toast Bowls

Preparation time: 10 minutes
Cooking time: 5 hours
Servings: 4

Ingredients:

- 1 and 1/2 cups almond milk
- 1 cup coconut cream
- 1 tablespoon vanilla extract
- 1/2 tablespoon cinnamon powder
- 2 tablespoons maple syrup
- 1/4 cup spenda
- 2 apples, cored and cubed
- 1/2 cup cranberries, dried
- 1 pound vegan bread, cubed
- Cooking spray

Directions:

1. Spray your crock pot with some cooking spray and add the bread.
2. Also, add cranberries and apples and stir gently.
3. Also, add cranberries and apples and stir gently.
4. Stir, cover and cook on Low for 5 hours.
5. Divide into bowls and serve right away.

Enjoy!

Nutrition:

- Calories 140
- Fat 2
- Fiber 3
- Carbs 6
- Protein 2

Banana and Coconut Oatmeal

Preparation time: 10 minutes
Cooking time: 7 hours
Servings: 6

Ingredients:

- 2 cups bananas, peeled and sliced
- 28 ounces canned coconut milk
- 1 cup steel cut oats
- 1/2 cup water
- 2 tablespoons palm sugar
- 1 and 1/2 tablespoons coconut butter
- 1/4 teaspoon nutmeg, ground
- 1/2 teaspoon cinnamon powder
- 1 tablespoon flax seed, ground
- 1/2 teaspoon vanilla extract
- A pinch of sea salt
- Chopped walnuts for serving
- Cooking spray

Directions:

1. Grease your crock pot with cooking spray and add coconut milk.
2. Also, add bananas, oats, water, palm sugar, coconut butter, cinnamon, nutmeg, flax seed and a pinch of salt. Stir, cover and cook on Low for 7 hours. Divide into bowls and serve with chopped walnuts on top.

Enjoy!

Nutrition:

- Calories 150
- Fat 2
- Fiber 1
- Carbs 5
- Protein 7

Maple and Pear Breakfast

Preparation time: 10 minutes
Cooking time: 9 hours
Servings: 2

Ingredients:

- 1 pear, cored and chopped
- 1/4 teaspoon maple extract
- 2 cups coconut milk
- 1/2 cup steel cut oats
- 1/2 teaspoon vanilla extract
- 1 tablespoon stevia
- 1/4 cup walnuts, chopped for serving
- Cooking spray

Directions:

3. Spray your Crock Pot with some cooking spray and add coconut milk.
4. Also, add maple extract, oats, pear, stevia and vanilla extract, stir, cover and cook on Low for 9 hours.
5. Stir your oatmeal again, divide it into breakfast bowls and serve with chopped walnuts on top.

Enjoy!

Nutrition:

- Calories 150
- Fat 3
- Fiber 2
- Carbs 6
- Protein 6

Cherry Oatmeal

Preparation time: 10 minutes
Cooking time: 8 hours and 10 minutes
Servings: 4

Ingredients:

- 2 cups almond milk
- 2 cups water
- 1 cup steel cut oats
- 2 tablespoons cocoa powder

For the sauce:

- 2 tablespoons water
- 1 and 1/2 cups cherries, pitted and chopped

- 1/3 cup cherries, pitted
- 1/4 cup maple syrup
- 1/2teaspoon almond extract

- 1/4 teaspoon almond extract

Directions:

1. Put the almond milk in your crock pot.
2. Add 2 cups water, oats, cocoa powder, 1/3 cup cherries, maples syrup and 1/2 teaspoon almond extract.
3. Stir, cover and cook on Low for 8 hours.
4. In a small pan, mix 2 tablespoons water with 1 and 1/2 cups cherries and 1/4 teaspoon almond extract, stir well, bring to a simmer over medium heat and cook for 10 minutes until it thickens.
5. Divide oatmeal into breakfast bowls, top with the cherries sauce and serve.

Enjoy!

Nutrition:

- Calories 150
- Fat 1
- Fiber 2

- Carbs 6
- Protein 5

Breakfast Enchiladas

Preparation time: 10 minutes
Cooking time: 3 hours
Servings: 4

Ingredients:

- 10 ounces spinach
- 16 ounces canned black beans, drained
- 1 cup corn
- 2 cups cashew cheese, shredded
- 1/2 teaspoon cumin, ground
- A pinch of sea salt
- Black pepper to the taste
- 3 and 1/2 cups vegan salsa
- 4 corn tortillas
- 4 radishes, chopped
- 6 cups lettuce leaves, torn
- 1 small cucumber, chopped
- 1 small tomato, chopped
- 3 tablespoons lime juice
- 2 tablespoons olive oil

Directions:

1. Spread half of the salsa in your crock pot.
2. Add beans, corn, spinach, cumin, half of the cashew cheese, salt and pepper and stir.
3. Top with the rest of the salsa and the rest of the cashew cheese, cover and cook on Low for 3 hours.
4. Divide this mix on warm corn tortillas, wrap and divide between plates.
5. In a bowl, mix cucumber with radishes, tomatoes, lettuce, lime juice and olive oil and toss to coat.
6. Serve enchiladas with cucumber and tomatoes mix on the side.

Enjoy!

Nutrition:

- Calories 160
- Fat 3
- Fiber 4
- Carbs 10
- Protein 6

Blueberry Butter

Preparation time: 10 minutes
Cooking time: 6 hours
Servings: 12

Ingredients:

- 5 cups blueberries puree
- 2 teaspoons cinnamon powder
- Zest from 1 lemon
- 1 cup coconut sugar
- 1/2 teaspoon nutmeg, ground
- 1/4 teaspoon ginger, ground

Directions:

1. Put blueberries in your crock pot, cover and cook on Low for 1 hour.
2. Stir your berries puree, cover and cook on Low for 4 hours more.
3. Add sugar, ginger, nutmeg and lemon zest, stir and cook on High uncovered for 1 hour more.
4. Divide into jars, cover them and keep in a cold place until you serve it for breakfast.

Enjoy!

Nutrition:

- Calories 143
- Fat 2
- Fiber 3
- Carbs 3
- Protein 4

Lentils Sandwich

Preparation time: 10 minutes
Cooking time: 1 hour and 30 minutes
Servings: 4

Ingredients:

For the sauce:

- 1/2 cup blackstrap molasses
- 28 ounces canned tomatoes, crushed
- 6 ounces tomato paste
- 1/4 cup white vinegar
- 2 tablespoons apple cider vinegar
- 1 sweet onion, chopped
- 3 garlic cloves, minced
- 1 teaspoon dry mustard
- 1 tablespoon coconut sugar
- 1/4 teaspoon red pepper flakes
- A pinch of sea salt
- 1/4 teaspoon liquid smoke
- A pinch of cayenne
- 4 cups green lentils, cooked and drained

Directions:

1. Put molasses in your crock pot.
2. Add tomatoes, tomato paste, vinegar, apple cider vinegar, onion, garlic, mustard, sugar, salt, pepper flakes, cayenne and liquid smoke.
3. Stir everything, cover your crock pot and cook on High for 1 hour and 30 minutes.
4. Add lentils, stir gently, divide on vegan buns and serve for breakfast.

Enjoy!

Nutrition:

- Calories 150
- Fat 3
- Fiber 4
- Carbs 6
- Protein 7

Carrot and Zucchini Breakfast

Preparation time: 10 minutes
Cooking time: 8 hours
Servings: 4

Ingredients:

- 1 and 1/2 cups almond milk
- 1/2 cup steel cut oats
- A pinch of nutmeg, ground
- 1 small zucchini, grated
- 1 carrot, grated
- A pinch of cloves, ground
- 2 tablespoons agave nectar
- 1/2 teaspoon cinnamon powder
- 1/4 cup pecans, chopped

Directions:

1. Put the milk in your crock pot and mix with oats, zucchini, carrots, nutmeg, cloves, cinnamon and agave nectar.
2. Stir, cover and cook on Low for 8 hours.
3. Add pecans, stir gently, divide into bowls and serve right away.

Enjoy!

Nutrition:

- Calories 120
- Fat 1
- Fiber 2
- Carbs 5
- Protein 8

Mexican Breakfast

Preparation time: 10 minutes
Cooking time: 2 hours
Servings: 4

Ingredients:

- 1 cup brown rice
- 1 cup onion, chopped
- 2 cups veggie stock
- 1 red bell pepper, chopped
- 1 green bell pepper, chopped
- 4 ounces canned green chilies, chopped
- 15 ounces canned black beans, drained
- A pinch of salt
- Black pepper to the taste

For the salsa:

- 3 tablespoons lime juice
- 1 avocado, pitted, peeled and cubed
- 1/2 cup cilantro, chopped
- 1/2 cup green onions, chopped
- 1/2 cup tomato, chopped
- 1 poblano pepper, chopped
- 2 tablespoons olive oil
- 1/2 teaspoon cumin

Directions:

1. Put the stock in your crock pot. Add rice, onions and beans, stir, cover and cook on High for 1 hour and 30 minutes.
2. Add chilies, red and green bell peppers, a pinch of salt and black pepper, stir, cover again and cook on High for 3 o minutes more.
3. Meanwhile, in a bowl, mix avocado with green onions, tomato, poblano pepper, cilantro, oil, cumin, a pinch of salt, black pepper and lime juice and stir really well.
4. Divide rice mix into bowls; top each with the salsa you've just made and serve. Enjoy!

Nutrition:

- Calories 140
- Fat 2
- Fiber 2
- Carbs 5
- Protein 5

Pumpkin Breakfast Delight

Preparation time: 10 minutes
Cooking time: 6 hours
Servings: 4

Ingredients:

- 4 and 1/2cups water
- 1 and1/2 cups pumpkin puree
- 1 and 1/2 cups steel cut oats
- 1 teaspoon allspice
- 2 teaspoons cinnamon
- 1 teaspoon vanilla extract
- 1/2 cup coconut sugar
- 1/4 cup pecans, chopped
- 1 tablespoon cinnamon powder

Directions:

1. In your crock pot, mix water with pumpkin puree, oats, allspice, cinnamon and vanilla extract.
2. Stir, cover and cook on Low for 6 hours.
3. In a bowl, mix cinnamon with coconut sugar and pecans and stir.
4. Divide oats into bowls, sprinkle pecans mix on top and serve.

Enjoy!

Nutrition:

- Calories 140
- Fat 3
- Fiber 2
- Carbs 7
- Protein 6

Tofu Burrito

Preparation time: 10 minutes
Cooking time: 8 hours
Servings: 4

Ingredients:

- 15 ounces canned black beans, drained
- 2 tablespoons onions, chopped
- 7 ounces tofu, drained and crumbled
- 2 tablespoons green bell pepper, chopped
- 1/2 teaspoon turmeric
- 3/4 cup water
- 1/4 teaspoon smoked paprika
- 1/4 teaspoon cumin, ground
- 1/4 teaspoon chili powder
- A pinch of salt and black pepper
- 4 gluten free whole wheat tortillas serving
- Avocado, chopped for serving
- Salsa for serving

Directions:

1. Put black beans in your crock pot.
2. Add onions, tofu, bell pepper, turmeric, water, paprika, cumin, chili powder, a pinch of salt and pepper, stir, cover and cook on Low for 8 hours.
3. Divide this on each tortilla, add avocado and salsa, wrap, arrange on plates and serve.

Enjoy!

Nutrition:

- Calories 130
- Fat 4
- Fiber 2
- Carbs 5
- Protein 4

Cranberry French Toast

Preparation time: 10 minutes
Cooking time: 5 hours
Servings: 4

Ingredients:

- 1 tablespoon chia seeds
- 1/2 tablespoon agave nectar
- 1 cup almond milk
- 1/2 teaspoon vanilla extract
- 1/2 teaspoon cinnamon powder
- 4 vegan bread slices, cubed
- 1 tablespoon coconut oil

Directions:

1. Add coconut oil to your crock pot, also add bread cubes and toss a bit.
2. Also add milk, agave nectar, chia seeds, vanilla extract and cinnamon, toss, cover and cook on Low for 5 hours.
3. Divide into bowls and serve for breakfast.

Enjoy!

Nutrition:

- Calories 231
- Fat 4
- Fiber 7
- Carbs 14
- Protein 4

Blueberries Oatmeal

Preparation time: 10 minutes
Cooking time: 8 hours
Servings: 4

Ingredients:

- 1 cup blueberries
- 1 cup steel cut oats
- 1 cup coconut milk
- 2 tablespoons agave nectar
- 1/2 teaspoon vanilla extract
- Coconut flakes for serving
- Cooking spray

Directions:

1. Spray your crock pot with cooking spray, add oats, milk, agave nectar, vanilla and blueberries, toss, cover and cook on Low for 8 hours.
2. Stir your oatmeal one more time, divide into bowls, sprinkle coconut flakes all over and serve.

Enjoy!

Nutrition:

- Calories 182
- Fat 6
- Fiber 8
- Carbs 9
- Protein 6

Incredible Rice Pudding

Preparation time: 10 minutes
Cooking time: 3
hours Servings: 2

Ingredients:

- 1/2 cup coconut sugar
- 2 cups almond milk
- 1/2 cup brown rice
- 1 teaspoon vanilla extract
- 1 tablespoons flax seed meal
- 1/2 cup raisins
- 1 teaspoon cinnamon powder

Directions:

1. Put the milk in your crock pot.
2. Add rice and sugar and stir well.
3. Also, add flaxseed meal, raisins, vanilla and cinnamon, stir, cover and cook on Low for 2 hours.
4. Stir your pudding again, cover and cook on Low for 1 more hour.
5. Divide into bowls and serve.

Enjoy!

Nutrition:

- Calories 160
- Fat 2
- Fiber 3
- Carbs 8
- Protein 12

Vanilla Oatmeal

Preparation time: 10 minutes
Cooking time: 6 hours
Servings: 4

Ingredients:

- 3 cups water
- 3 cups almond milk
- 1 and 1/2 cups steel oats
- 4 dates, pitted and chopped
- 1 teaspoon cinnamon, ground
- 2 tablespoons coconut sugar
- 1/2 teaspoon ginger powder
- A pinch of nutmeg, ground
- A pinch of cloves, ground
- 1 teaspoon vanilla extract

Directions:

1. Put water and milk in your crock pot and stir.
2. Add oats, dates, cinnamon, sugar, ginger, nutmeg, cloves and vanilla extract, stir, cover and cook on Low for 6 hours.
3. Divide into bowls and serve for breakfast.

Enjoy!

Nutrition:

- Calories 120
- Fat 1
- Fiber 2
- Carbs 3
- Protein 5

Breakfast Fajitas

Preparation time: 10 minutes
Cooking time: 2 hours
Servings: 8

Ingredients:

- 4 ounces canned green chilies, chopped
- 3 tomatoes, chopped
- 1 green bell pepper, chopped
- 1 yellow onion, chopped
- 1 red bell pepper, chopped
- 2 teaspoons cumin, ground
- 1/2 teaspoon oregano, dried
- 2 teaspoons chili powder
- A pinch of sea salt
- Black pepper to the taste
- 8 whole wheat tortillas
- 2 avocados, pitted, peeled and chopped
- Cooking spray

Directions:

1. Grease your crock pot with some cooking spray and add chilies.
2. Also, add tomatoes, bell peppers, onion, cumin, oregano, chili powder, a pinch of salt and pepper, stir, cover and cook on High for 2 hours.
3. Stir again, divide veggies on tortillas, add avocado on top, wrap and serve for breakfast.

Enjoy!

Nutrition:

- Calories 140
- Fat 3
- Fiber 2
- Carbs 8
- Protein 12

Energy Bars

Preparation time: 10 minutes
Cooking time: 4 hours
Servings: 8

Ingredients:

- 1/2 teaspoon cinnamon
- 1 cup almond milk
- 1/3 cup quinoa
- 2 tablespoons chia seeds
- 1/3 cup apple, dried and chopped
- 1/2 cup raisins
- 2 tablespoons maple syrup
- 2 tablespoons almond butter, melted
- 1/3 cup almonds, roasted and chopped
- 2 tablespoons flax meal + 1 tablespoon water
- Cooking spray

Directions:

1. Grease your crock pot with cooking spray and add a parchment paper inside.
2. In a bowl, mix melted almond butter with maple syrup and whisk really well.
3. Add cinnamon and almond milk and whisk everything.
4. Add flax meal mixed with water and stir well again.
5. Transfer this to your crock pot, add quinoa, chia, apples and raisins, stir really well and press into the crock pot.
6. Cover and cook on Low for 4 hours.
7. Take quinoa sheet out of the crock pot using the parchment paper as handles, leave aside to cool down, slice and serve.

Enjoy!

Nutrition:

- Calories 140
- Fat 3
- Fiber 2
- Carbs 6
- Protein 5

Crock pot Breakfast Oats

Preparation time: 10 minutes
Cooking time: 8 hours and 10 minutes
Servings: 4

Ingredients:

- 2 cups almond milk
- 1 cup steel cut oats
- 2 cups water
- 1/3 cup cherries, dried
- 2 tablespoons cocoa powder
- 1/4 cup stevia
- 1/2 teaspoon almond extract

For the sauce:

- 2 tablespoons water
- 1 and 1/2 cup cherries
- 1/4 teaspoon almond extract

Directions:

1. In your crock pot, mix almond milk with oats, water, dried cherries, cocoa powder, stevia and 1/2 teaspoon almond extract, stir, cover and cook on Low for 8 hours.
2. Meanwhile, in a small pot, mix 2 tablespoons water with 1 and 1/2 cups cherries and 1/4 teaspoon almond extract, stir, bring to a simmer over medium heat and cook for 10 minutes.
3. Divide oats into bowls, drizzle cherry sauce all over and serve.

Enjoy!

Nutrition:

- Calories 172
- Fat 7
- Fiber 7
- Carbs 12
- Protein 6

Cranberry Breakfast Quinoa

Preparation time: 10 minutes
Cooking time: 2 hours
Servings: 4

Ingredients:

- 1 cup quinoa
- 3 cups coconut water
- 1 teaspoon vanilla extract
- 3 teaspoons stevia
- 1/8 cup coconut flakes
- 1/4cup cranberries, dried
- 1/8 cup almonds, chopped

Directions:

1. In your crock pot, mix quinoa with coconut water, vanilla, stevia, coconut flakes, almonds and cranberries, toss, cover and cook on High for 2 hours.
2. Stir quinoa mix one more time, divide into bowls and serve for breakfast.
Enjoy!

Nutrition:

- Calories 246
- Fat 5
- Fiber 5
- Carbs 30
- Protein 7

Pear Oatmeal

Preparation time: 10 minutes
Cooking time: 7 hours
Servings: 3

Ingredients:

- 2 cups coconut milk
- 1/2 cup steel cut oats
- 1/2 teaspoon vanilla extract
- 1 pear, chopped
- 1/2 teaspoon maple extract
- 1 tablespoon stevia

Directions:

1. In your crock pot, mix coconut milk with oats, vanilla, pear, maple extract and stevia, stir, cover and cook on Low for 7 hours.
2. Divide into bowls and serve for breakfast.

Enjoy!

Nutrition:

- Calories 200
- Fat 5
- Fiber 7
- Carbs 14
- Protein 4

Chia Pudding

Preparation time: 10 minutes
Cooking time: 2 hours
Servings: 4

Ingredients:

- 1/2 cup coconut chia granola
- 1/2 cup chia seeds
- 2 cups coconut milk
- 2 tablespoons coconut, shredded and unsweetened
- 1/4 cup maple syrup
- 1/2 teaspoon cinnamon powder
- 2 teaspoons cocoa powder
- 1/2 teaspoon vanilla extract

Directions:

1. In your crock pot, mix chia granola with chia seeds, coconut milk, coconut, maple syrup, cinnamon, cocoa powder and vanilla, toss, cover and cook on High for 2 hours.
2. Divide chia pudding into bowls and serve for breakfast.

Enjoy!

Nutrition:

- Calories 261
- Fat 4
- Fiber 8
- Carbs 10
- Protein 4

Carrot Oatmeal

Preparation time: 10 minutes
Cooking time: 7 hours
Servings: 4

Ingredients:

- 2 cups coconut milk
- 1/2 cup steel cut oats
- 1 cup carrots, shredded
- 1 teaspoon cardamom, ground
- 1/2 teaspoon agave nectar
- A pinch of saffron
- Cooking spray

Directions:

1. Spray your crock pot with cooking spray, add milk, oats, carrots, cardamom and agave nectar, stir, cover and cook on Low for 7 hours.
2. Stir oatmeal again, divide into bowls, sprinkle saffron on top and serve for breakfast.

Enjoy!

Nutrition:

- Calories 182
- Fat 7
- Fiber 4
- Carbs 8
- Protein 3

Coconut Porridge

Preparation time: 10 minutes
Cooking time: 7 hours
Servings:4

Ingredients:

- 4 ounces jumbo rolled oats
- 13 ounces canned coconut milk
- 1/4 teaspoon cinnamon powder
- 1 teaspoon coconut oil
- 7 ounces canned mango and pineapple chunks

Directions:

1. Put the mill in your crock pot.
2. Add oats and cinnamon, stir, cover and cook on Low for 7 hours.
3. Stir your porridge and divide into bowls.
4. Heat up a pan with the oil over medium high heat, add mango and pineapple pieces, stir for about 1 minute and divide this on top of your porridge bowls.

Enjoy!

Nutrition:

- Calories 240
- Fat 3
- Fiber 3
- Carbs 8
- Protein 10

Rice Porridge

Preparation time: 10 minutes
Cooking time: 8 hours
Servings: 6

Ingredients:

- 1 apple, cored and cubed
- 6 cups water
- 1 cup brown rice
- 1/2 cup coconut, shredded
- 1/8 cup raisins
- 1/4 teaspoon cinnamon powder
- 1/2teaspoon pumpkin pie spice
- 1 tablespoon peanut butter
- Stevia to the taste

Directions:

1. Put the water in your crock pot.
2. Add rice, apple, coconut, raisins, cinnamon and pumpkin pie spice.
3. Stir, cover and cook on low for 8 hours.
4. Stir your porridge, divide it into bowls and top with peanut butter and stevia.
5. Stir your porridge again before serving.

Enjoy!

Nutrition:

- Calories 245
- Fat 4
- Fiber 3
- Carbs 7
- Protein 10

Breakfast Casserole

Preparation time: 10 minutes
Cooking time: 4 hours
Servings: 4

Ingredients:

- 2 teaspoons onion powder
- 3/4cup cashews, soaked for 30 minutes and drained
- 1/4 cup nutritional yeast
- 1 teaspoon garlic powder
- 1/2 teaspoon sage, dried
- Salt and black pepper to the taste
- 1 yellow onion, chopped
- 2 tablespoons parsley, chopped
- 3 garlic cloves, minced
- 1 tablespoon olive oil
- 4 red potatoes, cubed
- 1/2 teaspoon red pepper flakes

Directions:

1. In your blender, mix cashews with onion powder, garlic powder, nutritional yeast, sage, salt and pepper and pulse really well.
2. Add oil to your crock pot.
3. Arrange potatoes, pepper flakes, garlic, onion, salt, pepper and parsley and toss well.
4. Add cashews sauce, toss, cover and cook on High for 4 hours.
5. Arrange on plates and serve for breakfast.

Enjoy!

Nutrition:

- Calories 218
- Fat 6
- Fiber 6
- Carbs 14
- Protein 5

Banana Oatmeal

Preparation time: 10 minutes
Cooking time: 8 hours
Servings: 4

Ingredients:

- 1 banana, peeled and mashed
- 1 cup steel cut oats
- 2 cups almond milk
- 2 cups water
- 1/4 cup walnuts, chopped
- 2 tablespoons flax seed meal
- 2 teaspoons cinnamon powder
- 1 teaspoon vanilla extract
- 1/2 teaspoon nutmeg, ground

Directions:

1. In your crock pot mix oats with almond milk, water, walnuts, flaxseed meal, cinnamon, vanilla and nutmeg, stir, cover and cook on Low for 8 hours.
2. Stir oatmeal one more time, divide into bowls and serve for breakfast.

Enjoy!

Nutrition:

- Calories 291
- Fat 7
- Fiber 6
- Carbs 42
- Protein 11

Quinoa And Oats

Preparation time: 10 minutes
Cooking time: 7 hours
Servings: 6

Ingredients:

- 1/2 cup quinoa
- 1 and 1/2 cups steel cut oats
- 4 tablespoons stevia
- 4 and 1/2 cups almond milk
- 2 tablespoons maple syrup
- 1 and 1/2 teaspoons vanilla extract
- Strawberries, halved for serving
- Cooking spray

Directions:

1. Spray your crock pot with cooking spray, add oats, quinoa, stevia, almond milk, maple syrup and vanilla extract, toss, cover and cook on Low for 7 hours.
2. Divide into bowls, add strawberries on top and serve for breakfast.

Enjoy!

Nutrition:

- Calories 267
- Fat 5
- Fiber 8
- Carbs 28
- Protein 5

Almond Butter Oatmeal

Preparation time: 10 minutes
Cooking time: 10 hours
Servings: 2

Ingredients:

- 1/2 cup steel cut oats
- 1/2 cup almond milk
- Seeds from 1 vanilla bean
- 1 cup water
- 4 tablespoons almond butter
- Stevia to the taste

Directions:

1. In 2 heatproof containers, divide oats, almond milk, vanilla seeds, water, stevia and almond butter and stir.
2. Arrange containers in your crock pot, fill crock pot halfway with water, cover and cook on Low for 10 hours.
3. Serve warm for breakfast.

Enjoy!

Nutrition:

- Calories 182
- Fat 3
- Fiber 7
- Carbs 18
- Protein 4

Banana Bread

Preparation time: 10 minutes
Cooking time: 4 hours
Servings: 6

Ingredients:

- 3 bananas, peeled and mashed
- 1 teaspoon baking powder
- 1/2 teaspoon baking soda
- 2 cups whole wheat flour
- 1 cup palm sugar
- 2 tablespoons flax meal + 1 tablespoon water
- 1/2 cup coconut butter, melted

Directions:

1. In a bowl, mix sugar with flour, baking soda and baking powder and stir.
2. Add flax meal mixed with the water, butter and bananas, stir really well and pour the mix into a greased round pan that fits your crock pot.
3. Arrange the pan into your crock pot, cover and cook on Low for 4 hours.
4. Leave your bread to cool down, slice and serve it for breakfast.

Enjoy!

Nutrition:

- Calories 160
- Fat 3
- Fiber 3
- Carbs 7
- Protein 6

Pumpkin Pecan Oatmeal

Preparation time: 10 minutes
Cooking time: 8 hours
Servings: 4

Ingredients:

- 1 and 1/2 cups water
- 1/2 cup pumpkin puree
- 1 teaspoon pumpkin pie spice
- 3 tablespoons stevia
- 1/2 cup steel cut oats
- 1/4 cup pecans, chopped

Directions:

1. In your crock pot mix water with oats, pumpkin puree, pumpkin spice and stevia, stir, cover and cook on Low for 8 hours.
2. Sprinkle pecans on top, toss, divide into bowls and serve for breakfast.

Enjoy!

Nutrition:

- Calories 211
- Fat 4
- Fiber 7
- Carbs 8
- Protein 3

Apple and Pears Breakfast

Preparation time: 10 minutes
Cooking time: 6 hours
Servings: 6

Ingredients:

- 4 apples, cored, peeled and cut into medium chunks
- 1 teaspoon lemon juice
- 4 pears, cored, peeled and cut into medium chunks
- 5 teaspoons stevia
- 1 teaspoon cinnamon powder
- 1 teaspoon vanilla extract
- 1/2 teaspoon ginger, ground
- 1/2 teaspoon cloves, ground
- 1/2 teaspoon cardamom, ground

Directions:

1. In your crock pot, mix apples with pears, lemon juice, stevia, cinnamon, vanilla extract, ginger, cloves and cardamom, stir, cover and cook on Low for 6 hours.
2. Divide into bowls and serve for breakfast.

Enjoy!

Nutrition:

- Calories 201
- Fat 3
- Fiber 7
- Carbs 19
- Protein 4

Fruity Breakfast

Preparation time: 10 minutes
Cooking time: 8 hours
Servings: 6

Ingredients:

- 1 cup apricots, dried and chopped
- 3/4 cup red quinoa
- 3/4 cup steel cut oats
- 2 tablespoons agave nectar
- 1/2 teaspoon vanilla bean paste
- 3/4 cup hazelnuts, toasted and chopped
- 6 cups water
- Chopped hazelnuts for serving

Directions:

1. In a bowl, mix quinoa with oats, vanilla bean paste, apricots, hazelnuts, agave nectar and water and stir well.
2. Pour this into your crock pot, cover and cook on Low for 8 hours.
3. Stir again everything, divide into bowls and serve with more chopped hazelnuts on top.

Enjoy!

Nutrition:

- Calories 251
- Fat 4
- Fiber 4
- Carbs 10
- Protein 7

Tofu Casserole

Preparation time: 10 minutes
Cooking time: 4 hours
Servings: 4

Ingredients:

- 1 teaspoon lemon zest, grated
- 14 ounces tofu, cubed
- 1 tablespoon lemon juice
- 2 tablespoons nutritional yeast
- 1 tablespoon apple cider vinegar
- 1 tablespoon olive oil
- 2 garlic cloves, minced
- 10 ounces spinach, torn
- 1/2 cup yellow onion, chopped
- 1/2 teaspoon basil, dried
- 8 ounces mushrooms, sliced
- Salt and black pepper to the taste
- 1/4 teaspoon red pepper flakes
- Cooking spray

Directions:

1. Spray your crock pot with some cooking spray and arrange tofu cubes on the bottom.
2. Add lemon zest, lemon juice, yeast, vinegar, olive oil, garlic, spinach, onion, basil, mushrooms, salt, pepper and pepper flakes, toss, cover and cook on Low for 4 hours.
3. Divide between plates and serve for breakfast.

Enjoy!

Nutrition:

- Calories 216
- Fat 6
- Fiber 8
- Carbs 12
- Protein 4

Vegan Frittata

Preparation time: 10 minutes
Cooking time: 6 hours
Servings: 4

Ingredients:

- 1 pound firm tofu, drained, pressed and crumbled
- 2 tablespoons olive oil
- 1/4 cup nutritional yeast
- 1 yellow onion, chopped
- 1/4 teaspoon turmeric powder
- 3 tablespoons garlic, minced
- 1 red bell pepper, chopped
- 1/2 cup kalamata olives, pitted and halved
- 1 teaspoon basil, dried
- 1 teaspoon oregano, dried
- 1 tablespoon lemon juice
- Salt and black pepper to the taste

Directions:

1. Add the oil to your crock pot and arrange crumbled tofu on the bottom.
2. Add yeast, onion, turmeric, garlic, bell pepper, olives, basil, oregano, lemon juice, salt and pepper, toss a bit, cover and cook on Low for 6 hours.
3. Divide frittata between plates and serve for breakfast.

Enjoy!

Nutrition:

- Calories 271
- Fat 4
- Fiber 7
- Carbs 20
- Protein 6

Breakfast Burrito

Preparation time: 10 minutes
Cooking time: 6 hours
Servings: 8

Ingredients:

- 16 ounces tofu, crumbled
- 1 green bell pepper, chopped
- 1/4 cup scallions, chopped
- 15 ounces canned black beans, drained
- 1 cup vegan salsa
- 1/2 cup water
- 1/4 teaspoon cumin, ground
- 1/2 teaspoon turmeric powder
- 1/2 teaspoon smoked paprika
- A pinch of salt and black pepper
- 1/4 teaspoon chili powder
- 3 cups spinach leaves, torn
- 8 vegan tortillas for serving

Directions:

1. In your crock pot, mix tofu with bell pepper, scallions, black beans, salsa, water, cumin, turmeric, paprika, salt, pepper and chili powder, stir, cover and cook on Low for 6 hours.
2. Add spinach, toss well, divide this on your vegan tortillas, roll, wrap them and serve for breakfast.

Enjoy!

Nutrition:

- Calories 211
- Fat 4
- Fiber 7
- Carbs 14
- Protein 4

Carrot And Zucchini Oatmeal

Preparation time: 10 minutes
Cooking time: 8 hours
Servings: 4

Ingredients:

- 1/2 cup steel cut oats
- 1 carrot, grated
- 1 and 1/2 cups almond milk
- 1/4 zucchini, grated
- A pinch of nutmeg, ground
- A pinch of cloves, ground
- 1/2 teaspoon cinnamon powder
- 2 tablespoons maple syrup
- 1/4 cup pecans, chopped
- 1 teaspoon vanilla extract

Directions:

1. In your crock pot, mix oats with carrot, zucchini, almond milk, cloves, nutmeg, cinnamon, maple syrup, pecans and vanilla extract, stir, cover and cook on Low for 8 hours.
2. Stir your oatmeal one more time, divide into bowls and serve.
Enjoy!

Nutrition:

- Calories 215
- Fat 4
- Fiber 7
- Carbs 12
- Protein 7

Healthy Steel Cut Oats

Preparation time: 10 minutes
Cooking time: 4 hours
Servings: 6

Ingredients:

- 1 and 1/2 cups water
- 1 and 1/2 cups coconut milk
- 2 apples, cored, peeled and chopped
- 1 cup steel cut oats
- 1/2 teaspoon cinnamon powder
- 1/4 teaspoon nutmeg, ground
- 1/4 teaspoon allspice, ground
- 1/4 teaspoon ginger powder
- 1/4 teaspoon cardamom, ground
- 1 tablespoon flax seed, ground
- 2 teaspoons vanilla extract
- 2 teaspoons stevia
- Cooking spray

Directions:

1. Spray your crock pot with cooking spray, add apple pieces, milk, water, cinnamon, oats, allspice, nutmeg, cardamom, ginger, vanilla, flax seeds and stevia, stir, cover and cook on Low for 4 hours.
2. Stir oatmeal again, divide into bowls and serve.
Enjoy!

Nutrition:

- Calories 162
- Fat 3
- Fiber 7
- Carbs 8
- Protein 5

Vegan Scramble

Preparation time: 10 minutes
Cooking time: 8 hours
Servings: 4

Ingredients:

- 1 pound tofu, crumbled
- 1 pound white mushrooms, sliced
- 1 cup green onions, chopped
- 1 cup corn
- 1 tablespoon olive oil
- A pinch of salt and black pepper
- 1 zucchini, chopped
- 1/4 cup coconut aminos
- 1/2 cup nutritional yeast
- 3 pounds baby red potatoes, halved

Directions:

1. In your crock pot, mix oil with tofu, mushrooms, green onions, corn, salt, pepper, zucchini, aminos, yeast and potatoes, toss, cover and cook on Low for 8 hours.
2. Divide between plates and serve for breakfast.
Enjoy!

Nutrition:

- Calories 222
- Fat 5
- Fiber 8
- Carbs 12
- Protein 4

Apple Granola

Preparation time: 10 minutes
Cooking time: 4 hours
Servings: 3

Ingredients:

- 1/2 cup granola
- 1/2 cup bran flakes
- 2 green apples, cored, peeled and roughly chopped
- 1/4 cup apple juice
- 1/8 cup maple syrup
- 2 tablespoons cashew butter
- 1 teaspoon cinnamon powder
- 1/2 teaspoon nutmeg, ground

Directions:

1. In your crock pot, mix granola with bran flakes, apples, apple juice, maple syrup, cashew butter, cinnamon and nutmeg, toss, cover and cook on Low for 4 hours.
2. Divide apple granola into bowls and serve for breakfast.

Enjoy!

Nutrition:

- Calories 218
- Fat 6
- Fiber 9
- Carbs 17
- Protein 6

Chapter 4: Vegan Crock Pot Side Dish Recipes

Beans, Carrots and Spinach Side Dish

Preparation time: 10 minutes
Cooking time: 4 hours
Servings: 6

Ingredients:

- 5 carrots, sliced
- 1 and 1/2 cups great northern beans, dried, soaked overnight and drained
- 2 garlic cloves, minced
- 1 yellow onion, chopped
- Salt and black pepper to the taste
- 1/2 teaspoon oregano, dried
- 5 ounces baby spinach
- 4 and 1/2 cups veggie stock
- 2 teaspoons lemon peel, grated
- 3 tablespoons lemon juice
- 1 avocado, pitted, peeled and chopped
- 3/4 cup tofu, firm, pressed, drained and crumbled
- 1/4 cup pistachios, chopped

Directions:

1. In your crock pot, mix beans with onion, carrots, garlic, salt, pepper, oregano and veggie stock, stir, cover and cook on High for 4 hours.
2. Drain beans mix, return to your crock pot and reserve 1/4 cup cooking liquid.
3. Add spinach, lemon juice and lemon peel, stir and leave aside for 5 minutes.
4. Transfer beans, carrots and spinach mixture to a bowl, add pistachios, avocado, tofu and reserve cooking liquid, toss, divide between plates and serve as a side dish.

Enjoy!

Nutrition:

- Calories 319
- Fat 8
- Fiber 14
- Carbs 43
- Protein 17

Scalloped Potatoes

Preparation time: 10 minutes
Cooking time: 4 hours
Servings: 8

Ingredients:

- Cooking spray
- 2 pounds gold potatoes, halved and sliced
- 1 yellow onion, cut into medium wedges
- 10 ounces canned vegan potato cream soup
- 8 ounces coconut milk
- 1 cup tofu, crumbled
- 1/2 cup veggie stock
- Salt and black pepper to the taste
- 1 tablespoons parsley, chopped

Directions:

1. Coat your crock pot with cooking spray and arrange half of the potatoes on the bottom.
2. Layer onion wedges, half of the vegan cream soup, coconut milk, tofu, stock, salt and pepper.
3. Add the rest of the potatoes, onion wedges, cream, coconut milk, tofu and stock, cover and cook on High for 4 hours.
4. Sprinkle parsley on top, divide scalloped potatoes between plates and serve as a side dish.

Enjoy!

Nutrition:

- Calories 306
- Fat 14
- Fiber 4
- Carbs 30
- Protein 12

Wild Rice Mix

Preparation time: 10 minutes
Cooking time: 6 hours
Servings: 12

Ingredients:

- 40 ounces veggie stock
- 2 and 1/2 cups wild rice
- 1 cup carrot, shredded
- 4 ounces mushrooms, sliced
- 2 tablespoons olive oil
- 2 teaspoons marjoram, dried and crushed
- Salt and black pepper to the taste
- 2/3 cup dried cherries
- 1/2 cup pecans, toasted and chopped
- 2/3 cup green onions, chopped

Directions:

1. In your crock pot, mix stock with wild rice, carrot, mushrooms, oil, marjoram, salt, pepper, cherries, pecans and green onions, toss, cover and cook on Low for 6 hours.
2. Stir wild rice one more time, divide between plates and serve as a side dish.
Enjoy!

Nutrition:

- Calories 169
- Fat 5
- Fiber 3
- Carbs 28
- Protein 5

Barley and Squash Gratin

Preparation time: 10 minutes
Cooking time: 7 hours
Servings: 12

Ingredients:

- 2 pounds butternut squash, peeled and cubed
- 1 yellow onion, cut into medium wedges
- 10 ounces spinach
- 1 cup barley
- 14 ounces veggie stock
- 1/2 cup water
- A pinch of salt
- Black pepper to the taste
- 3 garlic cloves, minced

Directions:

1. Put squash pieces in your crock pot.
2. Add barley, spinach, stock, water, onion, garlic, salt and pepper, stir, cover and cook on Low for 7 hours.
3. Stir this mix again, divide between plates and serve.

Enjoy!

Nutrition:

- Calories 200
- Fat 3
- Fiber 7
- Carbs 13
- Protein 7

Mashed Potatoes

Preparation time: 10 minutes
Cooking time: 6 hours
Servings: 12

Ingredients:

- 3 pounds russet potatoes, peeled and cubed
- 6 garlic cloves, chopped
- 28 ounces veggie stock
- 1 bay leaf
- 1 cup coconut milk
- 1/4 cup coconut butter
- A pinch of sea salt
- White pepper to the taste

Directions:

1. Put potatoes in your crock pot.
2. Add stock, garlic and bay leaf, stir, cover and cook on Low for 6 hours.
3. Drain potatoes, discard bay leaf, return them to your crock pot and mash using a potato masher.
4. Meanwhile, put the coconut milk in a pot, stir and heat up over medium heat.
5. Add coconut butter and stir until it dissolves.
6. Add this to your mashed potatoes, season with a pinch of salt and white pepper, stir well, divide between plates and serve as a side dish.

Enjoy!

Nutrition:

- Calories 1535
- Fat 4
- Fiber 2
- Carbs 10
- Protein 4

Beans and Lentils

Preparation time: 10 minutes
Cooking time: 7 hours and 10 minutes
Servings: 6

Ingredients:

- 2 tablespoons thyme, chopped
- 1 tablespoon olive oil
- 1 cup yellow onion, chopped
- 5 cups water 5 garlic cloves, minced
- 3 tablespoons cider vinegar
- 1/2 cup tomato paste
- 1/2 cup maple syrup
- 3 tablespoons soy sauce
- 2 tablespoons Korean red chili paste
- 2 tablespoons dry mustard
- 1 and 1/2 cups great northern beans
- 1/2 cup red lentils

Directions:

1. Heat up a pan with the oil over medium high heat, add onion, stir and cook for 4 minutes.
2. Add garlic, thyme, vinegar and tomato paste, stir, cook for 5 minutes more and transfer to your crock pot.
3. Add lentils and beans to your crock pot and stir.
4. Also add water, maple syrup, mustard, chili paste and soy sauce, stir, cover and cook on High for 7 hours.
5. Stir beans mix again, divide between plates and serve.

Enjoy!

Nutrition:

- Calories 160
- Fat 2
- Fiber 4
- Carbs 7
- Protein 8

Sweet Potatoes Dish

Preparation time: 10 minutes
Cooking time: 6 hours
Servings: 6

Ingredients:

- 4 pounds sweet potatoes, peeled and sliced
- 1/2 cup orange juice
- 3 tablespoons palm sugar
- 1/2 teaspoon thyme, dried
- A pinch of sea salt
- Black pepper to the taste
- 1/2 teaspoon sage, dried
- 2 tablespoons olive oil

Directions:

1. Put the oil in your crock pot and add sweet potato slices.
2. In a bowl, mix orange juice with palm sugar, thyme, sage, a pinch of salt and black pepper and whisk well.
   Add this over potatoes, toss to coat, cover crock pot and cook on Low for 6 hours.
3. Stir sweet potatoes mix again, divide between plates and serve.

Enjoy!

Nutrition:

- Calories 160
- Fat 3
- Fiber 2
- Carbs 6
- Protein 9

Cauliflower And Broccoli Side Dish

Preparation time: 10 minutes
Cooking time: 3 hours
Servings: 10

Ingredients:

- 4 cups broccoli florets
- 4 cups cauliflower florets
- 14 ounces tomato paste
- 1 yellow onion, chopped
- 1 teaspoon thyme, dried
- Salt and black pepper to the taste
- 1/2 cup almonds, sliced

Directions:

1. In your crock pot, mix broccoli with cauliflower, tomato paste, onion, thyme, salt and pepper, toss, cover and cook on High for 3 hours.
2. Add almonds, toss, divide between plates and serve as a side dish.

Enjoy!

Nutrition:

- Calories 177
- Fat 12
- Fiber 2
- Carbs 10
- Protein 7

Collard Greens

Preparation time: 10 minutes
Preparation time: 10 minutes
Cooking time: 4 hours and 5 minutes
Servings: 4

Ingredients:

- 1 tablespoons olive oil
- 1 cup yellow onion, chopped
- 16 ounces collard greens
- 2 garlic cloves, minced
- A pinch of sea salt
- Black pepper to the taste
- 14 ounces veggie stock
- 1 bay leaf
- 1 tablespoon agave nectar
- 3 tablespoon balsamic vinegar

Directions:

1. Heat up a pan with the oil over medium high heat, add onion, stir and cook for 3 minutes. Add collard greens, stir, cook for 2 minutes more and transfer to your crock pot.
2. Add garlic, salt, pepper, stock and bay leaf, stir, cover and cook on Low for 4 hours.
3. In a bowl, mix vinegar with agave nectar and whisk well.
4. Add this to collard greens, stir, divide between plates and serve.
Enjoy!

Nutrition:

- Calories 130
- Fat 1
- Fiber 2
- Carbs 5
- Protein 3

Mexican Black Beans

Preparation time: 10 minutes
Cooking time: 10 hours
Servings: 4

Ingredients:

- 1 pound black beans, soaked overnight and drained
- A pinch of sea salt
- Black pepper to the taste
- 3 cups veggie stock
- 2 cups yellow onion, chopped
- 1 tablespoon canned chipotle chili pepper in adobo sauce
- 4 garlic cloves, minced
- 1 tablespoon lime juice
- 1/2 cup cilantro, chopped
- 1/2 cup pumpkin seeds

Directions:

1. Put the beans in your crock pot.
2. Add a pinch of salt, black pepper, onion, stock, garlic and chipotle chili in adobo sauce.
3. Stir, cover and cook on Low for 10 hours.
4. Add lime juice and mash beans a bit using a potato masher.
5. Add cilantro, stir gently, divide between plates and serve with pumpkin seeds on top.

Enjoy!

Nutrition:

- Calories 150
- Fat 3
- Fiber 4
- Carbs 7
- Protein 5

Black Eyed Peas

Preparation time: 10 minutes
Cooking time: 8 hours
Servings: 6

Ingredients:

- 3 cups black eyed peas
- A pinch of salt
- Black pepper to the taste
- 2 cups veggie stock
- 2 tablespoons jalapeno peppers, chopped
- 2 cups sweet onion, chopped
- 1/2 teaspoon thyme, dried
- 4 garlic cloves, minced
- 1 bay leaf
- Hot sauce to the taste

Directions:

1. Put the peas in your crock pot.
2. Add a pinch of salt, black pepper, stock, jalapenos, onion, garlic, thyme and bay leaf.
3. Stir everything, cover and cook on Low for 8 hours.
4. Drizzle hot sauce over peas, stir gently, divide between plates and serve.

Enjoy!

Nutrition:

- Calories 130
- Fat 2
- Fiber 4
- Carbs 7
- Protein 7

Creamy Corn

Preparation time: 10 minutes
Cooking time: 3 hours
Servings: 6

Ingredients:

- 50 ounces corn
- 1 cup almond milk
- 1 tablespoon stevia
- 8 ounces coconut cream
- A pinch of white pepper

Directions:

1. In your crock pot, mix corn with almond milk, stevia, cream and white pepper, toss, cover and cook on High for 3 hours.
2. Divide between plates and serve as a side dish.

Enjoy!

Nutrition:

- Calories 200
- Fat 5
- Fiber 7
- Carbs 12
- Protein 4

Flavored Beets

Preparation time: 10 minutes
Cooking time: 8 hours
Servings: 6

Ingredients:

- 6 beets, peeled and cut into wedges
- A pinch of sea salt
- Black pepper to the taste
- 2 tablespoons lemon juice
- 2 tablespoons olive oil
- 2 tablespoons agave nectar
- 1 tablespoon cider vinegar
- 1/2 teaspoon lemon rind, grated
- 2 rosemary sprigs

Directions:

1. Put the beets in your crock pot.
2. Add a pinch of salt, black pepper, lemon juice, oil, agave nectar, rosemary and vinegar. Stir everything, cover and cook on Low for 8 hours.
3. Add lemon rind, stir, divide between plates and serve.

Enjoy!

Nutrition:

- Calories 120
- Fat 1
- Fiber 2
- Carbs 6
- Protein 6

Eggplant And Kale Mix

Preparation time: 10 minutes
Cooking time: 2 hours
Servings: 6

Ingredients:

- 14 ounces canned roasted tomatoes and garlic
- 4 cups eggplant, cubed
- 1 yellow bell pepper, chopped
- 1 red onion, cut into medium wedges
- 4 cups kale leaves
- 2 tablespoons olive oil
- 1 teaspoon mustard
- 3 tablespoons red vinegar
- 1 garlic clove, minced
- A pinch of salt and black pepper
- 1/ 2cup basil, chopped

Directions:

1. In your crock pot, mix eggplant cubes with canned tomatoes, bell pepper and onion, toss, cover and cook on High for 2 hours.
2. Add kale, toss, cover crock pot and leave aside for now.
3. Meanwhile, in a bowl, mix oil with vinegar, mustard, garlic, salt and pepper and whisk well.
4. Add this over eggplant mix, also add basil, toss, divide between plates and serve as a side dish.

Enjoy!

Nutrition:

- Calories 251
- Fat 9
- Fiber 6
- Carbs 34
- Protein 8

Sweet Potatoes Side Dish

Preparation time: 10 minutes
Cooking time: 3 hours
Servings: 10

Ingredients:

- 4 pounds sweet potatoes, thinly sliced
- 3 tablespoons stevia
- 1/2 cup orange juice
- A pinch of salt and black pepper
- 1/2 teaspoon thyme, dried
- 1/2 teaspoon sage, dried
- 2 tablespoons olive oil

Directions:

1. Arrange potato slices on the bottom of your crock pot.
2. In a bowl, mix orange juice with salt, pepper, stevia, thyme, sage and oil and whisk well.
3. Add this over potatoes, cover crock pot and cook on High for 3 hours.
4. Divide between plates and serve as a side dish.

Enjoy!

Nutrition:

- Calories 189
- Fat 4
- Fiber 4
- Carbs 36
- Protein 4

Beets And Carrots

Preparation time: 10 minutes
Cooking time: 7 hours
Servings: 8

Ingredients:

- 2 tablespoons stevia
- 3/4 cup pomegranate juice
- 2 teaspoons ginger, grated
- 2 and $1/2 pounds beets, peeled and cut into wedges
- 12 ounces carrots, cut into medium wedges

Directions:

1. In your crock pot, mix beets with carrots, ginger, stevia and pomegranate juice, toss, cover and cook on Low for 7 hours.
2. Divide between plates and serve as a side dish.

Enjoy!

Nutrition:

- Calories 125
- Fat 0
- Fiber 4
- Carbs 28
- Protein 3

Orange Carrots

Preparation time: 10 minutes
Cooking time: 8 hours
Servings: 12

Ingredients:

- 3 pounds carrots, peeled and cut into medium pieces
- A pinch of sea salt
- Black pepper to the taste
- 2 tablespoons water 1/2 cup agave nectar
- 2 tablespoons olive oil
- 1/2 teaspoon orange rind, grated

Directions:

1. Put the oil in your crock pot and add the carrots.
2. In a bowl mix agave nectar with water and whisk well.
3. Add this to your crock pot as well.
4. Also, add a pinch of sea salt and black pepper, stir gently everything, cover and cook on Low for 8 hours.
5. Sprinkle orange rind all over, stir gently, divide on plates and serve.

Enjoy!

Nutrition:

- Calories 140
- Fat 2
- Fiber 2
- Carbs 4
- Protein 6

Chickpeas And Veggies

Preparation time: 10 minutes
Cooking time: 8 hour
Servings: 6

Ingredients:

- 30 ounces canned chickpeas, drained
- 2 tablespoons olive oil
- 2 tablespoons rosemary, chopped
- A pinch of salt and black pepper
- 2 cups cherry tomatoes, halved
- 2 garlic cloves, minced
- 1 cup corn
- 1 pound baby potatoes, peeled and halved
- 12 small baby carrots, peeled
- 28 ounces veggie stock
- 1 yellow onion, cut into medium wedges
- 4 cups baby spinach
- 8 ounces zucchini, sliced

Directions:

1. In your crock pot, mix chickpeas with oil, rosemary, salt, pepper, cherry tomatoes, garlic, corn, baby potatoes, baby carrots, onion, zucchini, spinach and stock, stir, cover and cook on Low for 8 hours.
2. Divide everything between plates and serve as a side dish.

Enjoy!

Nutrition:

- Calories 273
- Fat 7
- Fiber 11
- Carbs 38
- Protein 12

Wild Rice

Preparation time: 10 minutes
Cooking time: 6 hours
Servings: 12

Ingredients:

- 42 ounces veggie stock
- 1 cup carrot, shredded
- 2 and 1/2 cups wild rice
- 4 ounces mushrooms, sliced
- 2 tablespoons olive oil
- 2 teaspoons marjoram, dried
- A pinch of sea salt
- Black pepper to the taste
- 2/3 cup cherries, dried
- 1/2 cup pecans, chopped
- 2/3 cup green onions, chopped

Directions:

1. Put the stock in your crock pot.
2. Add rice, carrots, mushrooms, oil, salt, pepper marjoram.
3. Stir, cover and cook on Low for 6 hours.
4. Add cherries and green onions, stir, cover crock pot and leave it aside for 10 minutes.
5. Divide wild rice between plates and serve with chopped pecans on top.
Enjoy!

Nutrition:

- Calories 140
- Fat 2
- Fiber 3
- Carbs 6
- Protein 7

Thai Veggie Mix

Preparation time: 10 minutes
Cooking time: 3 hours
Servings: 8

Ingredients:

- 8 ounces yellow summer squash, peeled and roughly chopped
- 12 ounces zucchini, halved and sliced
- 2 cups button mushrooms, quartered
- 1 red sweet potatoes, chopped
- 2 leeks, sliced
- 2 tablespoons veggie stock
- 2 garlic cloves, minced
- 2 tablespoon Thai red curry paste
- 1 tablespoon ginger, grated
- 1/3 cup coconut milk
- 1/4cup basil, chopped

Directions:

1. In your crock pot, mix zucchini with summer squash, mushrooms, red pepper, leeks, garlic, stock, curry paste, ginger, coconut milk and basil, toss, cover and cook on Low for 3 hours.
2. Stir your Thai mix one more time, divide between plates and serve as a side dish. Enjoy!

Nutrition:

- Calories 69
- Fat 2
- Fiber 2
- Carbs 8
- Protein 2

Rustic Mashed Potatoes

Preparation time: 10 minutes
Cooking time: 4 hours
Servings: 6

Ingredients:

- 6 garlic cloves, peeled
- 3 pounds gold potatoes, peeled and cubed
- 1 bay leaf
- 1 cup coconut milk
- 28 ounces veggie stock
- 3 tablespoons olive oil
- Salt and black pepper to the taste

Directions:

1. In your crock pot, mix potatoes with stock, bay leaf, garlic, salt and pepper, cover and cook on High for 4 hours.
2. Drain potatoes and garlic, return them to your crock pot and mash using a potato masher.
3. Add oil and coconut milk, whisk well, divide between plates and serve as a side dish.

Enjoy!

Nutrition:

- Calories 135
- Fat 5
- Fiber 1
- Carbs 20
- Protein 3

Potatoes Mix

Preparation time: 10 minutes
Cooking time: 7 hours
Servings: 10

Ingredients:

- 2 green apples, cored and cut into wedges
- 3 pounds sweet potatoes, peeled and cut into medium wedges
- 1 cup coconut cream
- 1/2 cup dried cherries
- 1 cup apple butter
- 1 and 1/2 teaspoon pumpkin pie spice

Directions:

1. In your crock pot, mix sweet potatoes with green apples, cream, cherries, apple butter and spice, toss, cover and cook on Low for 7 hours.
2. Toss, divide between plates and serve as a side dish.

Enjoy!

Nutrition:

- Calories 351
- Fat 8
- Fiber 5
- Carbs 48
- Protein 2

Squash And Spinach Mix

Preparation time: 10 minutes
Cooking time: 3 hours and 30 minutes
Servings: 12

Ingredients:

- 10 ounces spinach, torn
- 2 pounds butternut squash, peeled and cubed
- 1 cup barley
- 1 yellow onion, chopped
- 14 ounces veggie stock
- 1/2 cup water
- A pinch of salt and black pepper to the taste
- 3 garlic cloves, minced

Directions:

1. In your crock pot, mix squash with spinach, barley, onion, stock, water, salt, pepper and garlic, toss, cover and cook on High for 3 hours and 30 minutes.
2. Divide squash mix on plates and serve as a side dish.

Enjoy!

Nutrition:

- Calories 196
- Fat 3
- Fiber 7
- Carbs 36
- Protein 7

Glazed Carrots

Preparation time: 10 minutes
Cooking time: 4 hours
Servings: 10

Ingredients:

- 1 pound parsnips, cut into medium chunks
- 2 pounds carrots, cut into medium chunks
- 2 tablespoons orange peel, shredded
- 1 cup orange juice
- 1/2 cup orange marmalade
- 1/2 cup veggie stock
- 1 tablespoon tapioca, crushed
- A pinch of salt and black pepper
- 3 tablespoons olive oil
- 1/4 cup parsley, chopped

Directions:

1. In your crock pot, mix parsnips with carrots.
2. In a bowl, mix orange peel with orange juice, stock, orange marmalade, tapioca, salt and pepper, whisk and add over carrots.
3. Cover crock pot and cook everything on High for 4 hours.
4. Add parsley, toss, divide between plates and serve as a side dish.

Enjoy!

Nutrition:

- Calories 159
- Fat 4
- Fiber 4
- Carbs 30
- Protein 2

Mushroom And Peas Risotto

Preparation time: 10 minutes
Cooking time: 1 hour and 30 minutes
Servings: 8

Ingredients:

- 1 shallot, chopped
- 8 ounces white mushrooms, sliced
- 3 tablespoons olive oil
- 1 teaspoon garlic, minced
- 1 and 3/4 cup white rice
- 4 cups veggie stock
- 1 cup peas
- Salt and black pepper to the taste

Directions:

1. In your crock pot, mix oil with shallot, mushrooms, garlic, rice, stock, peas, salt and pepper, stir, cover and cook on High for 1 hour and 30 minutes.
2. Stir risotto one more time, divide between plates and serve as a side dish.

Enjoy!

Nutrition:

- Calories 254
- Fat 7
- Fiber 3
- Carbs 27
- Protein 7

Italian Veggie Side Dish

Preparation time: 10 minutes
Cooking time: 6 hours
Servings: 8

Ingredients:

- 38 ounces canned cannellini beans, drained
- 1 yellow onion, chopped
- 1/4 cup basil pesto
- 19 ounces canned fava beans, drained
- 4 garlic cloves, minced
- 1 and 1/2 teaspoon Italian seasoning, dried and crushed
- 1 tomato, chopped
- 15 ounces already cooked polenta, cut into medium pieces
- 2 cups spinach
- 1 cup radicchio, torn

Directions:

1. In your crock pot, mix cannellini beans with fava beans, basil pesto, onion, garlic, Italian seasoning, polenta, tomato, spinach and radicchio, toss, cover and cook on Low for 6 hours.
2. Divide between plates and serve as a side dish.

Enjoy!

Nutrition:

- Calories 364
- Fat 12
- Fiber 10
- Carbs 45
- Protein 21

Acorn Squash And Great Sauce

Preparation time: 10 minutes
Cooking time: 6 hours
Servings: 4

Ingredients:

- 2 acorn squash, halved, deseeded and cut into medium wedges
- 1/4 cup raisins
- 16 ounces cranberry sauce
- 1/4 cup orange marmalade
- A pinch of salt and black pepper
- 1/4 teaspoon cinnamon powder

Directions:

1. In your crock pot, mix squash with raisins, cranberry sauce, orange marmalade, salt, pepper and cinnamon powder, toss, cover and cook on Low for 6 hours.
2. Stir again, divide between plates and serve as a side dish.

Enjoy!

Nutrition:

- Calories 325
- Fat 6
- Fiber 3
- Carbs 28
- Protein 3

Potatoes Side Dish

Preparation time: 10 minutes
Cooking time: 3 hours
Servings: 12

Ingredients:

- 2 tablespoons olive oil
- 3 pounds new potatoes, halved
- 7 garlic cloves, minced
- 1 tablespoon rosemary, chopped
- A pinch of salt and black pepper

Directions:

1. In your crock pot, mix oil with potatoes, garlic, rosemary, salt and pepper, toss, cover and cook on High for 3 hours.
2. Divide between plates and serve as a side dish.

Enjoy!

Nutrition:

- Calories 102
- Fat 2
- Fiber 2
- Carbs 18
- Protein 2

Chapter 5: Vegan Crock Pot Snack And Appetizer Recipes

Sweet and Spicy Nuts

Preparation time: 10 minutes
Cooking time: 2 hours
Servings: 20

Ingredients:

- 1 cup almonds, toasted
- 1 cup cashews
- 1 cup pecans, halved and toasted
- 1 cup hazelnuts, toasted and peeled
- 1/2 cup palm sugar
- 1 teaspoon ginger, grated
- 1/3 cup coconut butter, melted
- 1/2 teaspoon cinnamon powder
- 1/4 teaspoon cloves, ground
- A pinch of salt
- A pinch of cayenne pepper

Directions:

1. Put almonds, pecans, cashews and hazelnuts in your crock pot.
2. Add palm sugar, coconut butter, ginger, salt, cayenne, cloves and cinnamon.
3. Stir well, cover and cook on Low for 2 hours.
4. Divide into bowls and serve as a snack.

Enjoy!

Nutrition:

- Calories 110
- Fat 3
- Fiber 2
- Carbs 5
- Protein 5

Corn Dip

Preparation time: 10 minutes
Cooking time: 2 hours and 15 minutes
Servings: 8

Ingredients:

- 2 jalapenos, chopped
- 45 ounces canned corn kernels, drained
- 1/2 cup coconut milk
- 1 and 1/4 cups cashew cheese, shredded
- A pinch of sea salt
- Black pepper to the taste
- 2 tablespoons chives, chopped
- 8 ounces tofu, cubed

Directions:

1. In your crock pot, mix coconut milk with cashew cheese, corn, jalapenos, tofu, salt and pepper, stir, cover and cook on Low for 2 hours.
2. Stir your corn dip really well, cover crock pot again and cook on High for 15 minutes.
3. Divide into bowls, sprinkle chives on top and serve as a vegan snack!

Enjoy!

Nutrition:

- Calories 150
- Fat 3
- Fiber 2
- Carbs 8
- Protein 10

Vegan Rolls

Preparation time: 10 minutes
Cooking time: 8 hours
Servings: 4

Ingredients:

- 1 cup brown lentils, cooked
- 1 green cabbage head, leaves separated
- 1/2 cup onion, chopped
- 1 cup brown rice, already cooked
- 2 ounces white mushrooms, chopped
- 1/4 cup pine nuts, toasted
- 1/4 cup raisins
- 2 garlic cloves, minced
- 2 tablespoons dill, chopped
- 1 tablespoon olive oil
- 25 ounces marinara sauce
- A pinch of salt and black pepper
- 1/4 cup water

Directions:

1. In a bowl, mix lentils with onion, rice, mushrooms, pine nuts, raisins, garlic, dill, salt and pepper and whisk well.
2. Arrange cabbage leaves on a working surface, divide lentils mix and wrap them well.
3. Add marinara sauce and water to your crock pot and stir.
4. Add cabbage rolls, cover and cook on Low for 8 hours.
5. Arrange cabbage rolls on a platter, drizzle sauce all over and serve.

Enjoy!

Nutrition:

- Calories 261
- Fat 6
- Fiber 6
- Carbs 12
- Protein 3

Chipotle Tacos

Preparation time: 10 minutes
Cooking time: 4 hours
Servings: 4

Ingredients:

- 30 ounces canned pinto beans, drained
- 3/4 cup chili sauce
- 3 ounces chipotle pepper in adobo sauce, chopped
- 1 cup corn
- 6 ounces tomato paste
- 1 tablespoon cocoa powder
- 1/2 teaspoon cinnamon, ground
- 1 teaspoon cumin, ground
- 8 vegan taco shells
- Chopped avocado, for serving

Directions:

1. Put the beans in your crock pot.
2. Add chili sauce, chipotle pepper, corn, tomato paste, cocoa powder, cinnamon and cumin.
3. Stir, cover and cook on Low for 4 hours. Divide beans and chopped avocado into taco shells and serve them.

Enjoy!

Nutrition:

- Calories 342
- Fat 3
- Fiber 6
- Carbs 12
- Protein 10

Black Eyed Peas Pate

Preparation time: 10 minutes
Cooking time: 5 hours
Servings: 5

Ingredients:

- 1 and 1/2 cups black-eyed peas
- 3 cups water
- 1 teaspoon Cajun seasoning
- 1/2 cup pecans, toasted
- 1/2 teaspoon garlic powder
- 1/2 teaspoon jalapeno powder
- A pinch of salt and black pepper
- 1/4 teaspoon liquid smoke
- 1/2 teaspoon Tabasco sauce

Directions:

1. In your crock pot, mix black-eyed pea with Cajun seasoning, salt, pepper and water, stir, cover and cook on High for 5 hours.
2. Drain, transfer to a blender, add pecans, garlic powder, jalapeno powder, Tabasco sauce, liquid smoke, more salt and pepper, pulse well and serve as an appetizer.

Enjoy!

Nutrition:

- Calories: 221
- Fat: 4
- Fiber: 7
- Carbs: 16
- Protein: 4

Eggplant Appetizer

Preparation time: 10 minutes
Cooking time: 7 hours
Servings: 4

Ingredients:

- 1 and 1/2 cups tomatoes, chopped
- 3 cups eggplant, cubed
- 2 teaspoons capers
- 6 ounces green olives, pitted and sliced
- 4 garlic cloves, minced
- 2 teaspoons balsamic vinegar
- 1 tablespoon basil, chopped
- Salt and black pepper to the taste

Directions:

1. In your crock pot, mix tomatoes with eggplant cubes, capers, green olives, garlic, vinegar, basil, salt and pepper, toss, cover and cook on Low for 7 hours.
2. Divide into small appetizer plates and serve as an appetizer.

Enjoy!

Nutrition:

- Calories 200
- Fat 6
- Fiber 5
- Carbs 9
- Protein 2

Spinach Dip

Preparation time: 10 minutes
Cooking time: 30 minutes
Servings: 4

Ingredients:

- 1/2 cup coconut cream
- 3/4 cup coconut yogurt
- 10 ounces spinach leaves
- 8 ounces water chestnuts, chopped
- 1 garlic clove, minced
- Black pepper to the taste

Directions:

1. In your crock pot, mix coconut cream with spinach, coconut yogurt, chestnuts, black pepper and garlic, stir, cover and cook on High for 30 minutes.
2. Blend using an immersion blender, divide into bowls and serve.

Enjoy!

Nutrition:

- Calories: 221
- Fat: 5
- Fiber: 7
- Carbs: 12
- Protein: 5

Onion Dip

Preparation time: 10 minutes
Cooking time: 8 hours
Servings: 6

Ingredients:

- 3 cups yellow onions, chopped
- A pinch of sea salt
- 2 tablespoons olive oil
- 1 tablespoon coconut butter
- 1 cup coconut milk
- 1/2 cup avocado mayonnaise
- A pinch of cayenne pepper

Directions:

1. Put the onions in your crock pot.
2. Add a pinch of salt, oil and coconut butter, stir well, cover and cook on High for 8 hours.
3. Drain excess liquid, transfer onion to a bowl, add coconut milk, avocado mayo and cayenne, stir really well and serve with potato chips on the side.

Enjoy!

Nutrition:

- Calories 200
- Fat 4
- Fiber 4
- Carbs 9
- Protein 7

Black Bean Appetizer Salad

Preparation time: 10 minutes
Cooking time: 4 hours
Servings: 7

Ingredients:

- 1 tablespoon coconut aminos
- 1/2 teaspoon cumin, ground
- 1 cup canned black beans
- 1 cup salsa
- 6 cups romaine lettuce leaves
- 1/2 cup avocado, peeled, pitted and mashed

Directions:

1. In your crock pot, mix black beans with salsa, cumin and aminos, stir, cover and cook on Low for 4 hours.
2. In a salad bowl, mix lettuce leaves with black beans mix and mashed avocado, toss and serve as an appetizer.

Enjoy!

Nutrition:

- Calories: 221
- Fat: 4
- Fiber: 7
- Carbs: 12
- Protein: 3

Great Bolognese Dip

Preparation time: 10 minutes
Cooking time: 5 hours
Servings: 7

Ingredients:

- 1/2 cauliflower head, riced in your blender
- 54 ounces canned tomatoes, crushed
- 10 ounces white mushrooms, chopped
- 2 cups carrots, shredded
- 2 cups eggplant, cubed
- 6 garlic cloves, minced
- 2 tablespoons agave nectar
- 2 tablespoons balsamic vinegar
- 2 tablespoons tomato paste
- 1 tablespoon basil, chopped
- 1 and 1/2 tablespoons oregano, chopped
- 1 and 1/2 teaspoons rosemary, dried
- A pinch of salt and black pepper

Directions:

1. In your crock pot, mix cauliflower rice with tomatoes, mushrooms, carrots, eggplant cubes, garlic, agave nectar, balsamic vinegar, tomato paste, rosemary, salt and pepper, stir, cover and cook on High for 5 hours.
2. Add basil and oregano, stir again, divide into bowls and serve as a dip.
Enjoy!

Nutrition:

- Calories: 251
- Fat: 7
- Fiber: 6
- Carbs: 10
- Protein: 6

Vegan Veggie Dip

Preparation time: 10 minutes
Cooking time: 7 hours
Servings: 4

Ingredients:

- 1 cup carrots, sliced
- 1 and 1/2 cups cauliflower florets
- 1/3 cup cashews
- 1/2 cup turnips, chopped
- 2 and 1/2 cups water
- 1 cup almond milk
- 1 teaspoon garlic powder
- 1/4 cup nutritional yeast
- 1/4 teaspoon smoked paprika
- 1/4 teaspoon mustard powder
- A pinch of salt

Directions:

1. In your crock pot, mix carrots with cauliflower, cashews, turnips and water, stir, cover and cook on Low for 7 hours.
2. Drain, transfer to a blender, add almond milk, garlic powder, yeast, paprika, mustard powder and salt, blend well and serve as a snack.

Enjoy!

Nutrition:

- Calories 291
- Fat 7
- Fiber 4
- Carbs 14
- Protein 3

Tofu Appetizer

Preparation time: 10 minutes
Cooking time: 7 hours
Servings: 6

Ingredients:

- 1/4 cup yellow onions, sliced
- 1 cup carrot, sliced
- 14 ounces firm tofu, cubed

For the sauce:

- 1/4 cup soy sauce
- 1/2 cup water
- 3 tablespoons agave nectar
- 3 tablespoons nutritional yeast
- 1 tablespoon garlic, minced
- 1 tablespoon ginger, minced
- 1/2 tablespoon rice vinegar

Directions:

1. In your crock pot, mix tofu with onion and carrots.
2. In a bowl, mix soy sauce with water, agave nectar, yeast, garlic, ginger and vinegar and whisk well.
3. Add this to crock pot, cover and cook on Low for 7 hours.
4. Divide into appetizer bowls and serve.

Enjoy!

Nutrition:

- Calories: 251
- Fat: 6
- Fiber: 8
- Carbs: 12
- Protein: 3

Artichoke Spread

Preparation time: 10 minutes
Cooking time: 2 hours
Servings: 8

Ingredients:

- 28 ounces canned artichokes, drained and chopped
- 10 ounces spinach
- 8 ounces coconut cream
- 1 yellow onion, chopped
- 2 garlic cloves, minced
- 3/4 cup coconut milk
- 1/2 cup tofu, pressed and crumbled
- 1/3 cup vegan avocado mayonnaise
- 1 tablespoon red vinegar
- A pinch of salt and black pepper

Directions:

1. In your crock pot, mix artichokes with spinach, coconut cream, onion, garlic, coconut milk, tofu, avocado mayo, vinegar, salt and pepper, stir well, cover and cook on Low for 2 hours.
2. Divide into bowls and serve as an appetizer.

Enjoy!

Nutrition:

- Calories: 355
- Fat: 24
- Fiber: 4
- Carbs: 19
- Protein: 13

Spinach Dip

Preparation time: 10 minutes
Cooking time: 4 hours
Servings: 12

Ingredients:

- 8 ounces baby spinach
- 1 small yellow onion, chopped
- 8 ounces vegan cashew mozzarella, shredded
- 8 ounces tofu, cubed
- 1 cup vegan cashew parmesan cheese, grated
- 1 tablespoon garlic, minced
- A pinch of cayenne pepper
- A pinch of sea salt
- Black pepper to the taste

Directions:

1. Put spinach in your crock pot. Add onion, cashew mozzarella, tofu, cashew parmesan, salt, pepper, cayenne and garlic.
2. Stir, cover and cook on Low for 2 hours.
3. Stir your dip well, cover and cook on Low for 2 more hours.
4. Divide your spinach dip into bowls and serve.

Enjoy!

Nutrition:

- Calories 200
- Fat 3
- Fiber 4
- Carbs 6
- Protein 8

Cashew And White Bean Spread

Preparation time: 10 minutes
Cooking time: 7 hours
Servings: 4

Ingredients:

- 1/2 cup white beans, dried
- 2 tablespoons cashews, soaked for 12 hours and blended
- 1 teaspoon apple cider vinegar
- 1 cup veggie stock
- 1 tablespoon water

Directions:

1. In your crock pot, mix beans with cashews and stock, stir, cover and cook on Low for 6 hours.
2. Drain, transfer to your food processor, add vinegar and water, pulse well, divide into bowls and serve as a spread.

Enjoy!

Nutrition:

- Calories 221
- Fat 6
- Fiber 5
- Carbs 19
- Protein 3

Butternut Squash Spread

Preparation time: 10 minutes
Cooking time: 6 hours
Servings: 4

Ingredients:

- 1/2 cup butternut squash, peeled and cubed
- 1/2 cup canned white beans, drained
- 1 tablespoon water
- 2 tablespoons coconut milk
- A pinch of rosemary, dried
- A pinch of sage, dried
- A pinch of salt and black pepper

Directions:

1. In your crock pot, mix beans with squash, water, coconut milk, sage, rosemary, salt and pepper, toss, cover and cook on Low for 6 hours.
2. Blend using an immersion blender, divide into bowls and serve cold as a party spread.

Enjoy!

Nutrition:

- Calories 182
- Fat 5
- Fiber 7
- Carbs 12
- Protein 5

Three Bean Dip

Preparation time: 10 minutes
Cooking time: 1 hours
Servings: 6

Ingredients:

- 1/2 cup salsa
- 2 cups canned refried beans
- 1 cup vegan nacho cheese
- 2 tablespoons green onions, chopped

Directions:

1. In your crock pot, mix refried beans with salsa, vegan nacho cheese and green onions, stir, cover and cook on High for 1 hour.
2. Divide into bowls and serve as a party snack.

Enjoy!

Nutrition:

- Calories: 262
- Fat: 5
- Fiber: 10
- Carbs: 20
- Protein: 3

Colored Stuffed Bell Peppers

Preparation time: 10 minutes
Cooking time: 4 hours
Servings: 5

Ingredients:

- 1 yellow onion, chopped
- 2 teaspoons olive oil
- 2 celery ribs, chopped
- 1 tablespoon chili powder
- 3 garlic cloves, minced
- 2 teaspoon cumin, ground
- 1 and 1/2 teaspoon oregano, dried
- 2 cups white rice, already cooked
- 1 cup corn
- 1 tomato chopped
- 7 ounces canned pinto beans, drained
- 1 chipotle pepper in adobo
- A pinch of salt and black pepper
- 5 colored bell peppers, tops and insides scooped out
- 1/2 cup vegan enchilada sauce

Directions:

1. Heat up a pan with the oil over medium high heat, add onion and celery, stir and cook for 5 minutes.
2. Add garlic, stir, cook for 1 minute more, take off heat and mix with chili, cumin and oregano.
3. Also add rice, corn, beans, tomato, salt, pepper and chipotle pepper and stir well.
4. Stuff bell peppers with this mix and place them in your crock pot.
5. Add enchilada sauce, cover and cook on Low for 4 hours.
6. Arrange stuffed bell peppers on a platter and serve them as an appetizer.

Enjoy!

Nutrition:

- Calories: 221
- Fat: 5
- Fiber: 4
- Carbs: 19
- Protein: 3

Candied Almonds

Preparation time: 10 minutes
Cooking time: 4 hours
Servings: 10

Ingredients:

- 3 tablespoons cinnamon powder
- 3 cups palm sugar
- 4 and 1/2 cups almonds, raw
- 1/4 cup water
- 2 teaspoons vanilla extract

Directions:

1. In a bowl, mix water with vanilla extract and whisk.
2. In another bowl, mix cinnamon with sugar and stir.
3. Dip almonds in water, then add them to the bowl with the cinnamon sugar.
4. Toss to coat really well, add almonds to your crock pot, cover and cook on Low for 4 hours, stirring often.
5. Divide into bowls and serve as a snack.

Enjoy!

Nutrition:

- Calories 150
- Fat 3
- Fiber 4
- Carbs 6
- Protein 8

Beans in Tomato Sauce

Preparation time: 10 minutes
Cooking time: 8 hours and 10 minutes
Servings: 6

Ingredients:

- 1 pound lima beans, soaked for 6 hours and drained
- 2 celery ribs, chopped
- 2 tablespoons olive oil
- 2 onions, chopped
- 2 carrots, chopped
- 4 tablespoons tomato paste
- 3 garlic cloves, minced
- A pinch of sea salt
- Black pepper to the taste
- 7 cups water
- 1 bay leaf
- 1 teaspoon oregano, dried
- 1/2 teaspoon thyme, dried
- A pinch of red pepper, crushed
- 1/4 cup parsley, chopped
- 1 cup cashew cheese, shredded

Directions:

1. Heat up a pan with the oil over medium high heat, add onions, stir and cook for 4 minutes.
2. Add garlic, celery, carrots, salt and pepper, stir, cook for $4-5$ minutes more and transfer to your crock pot.
3. Add beans, tomato paste, water, bay leaf, oregano, thyme and red pepper, stir, cover and cook on Low for 8 hours.
4. Add parsley, stir, divide into bowls and serve cold with cashew cheese on top.

Enjoy!

Nutrition:

- Calories 160
- Fat 3
- Fiber 7
- Carbs 9
- Protein 12

Chapter 6: Vegan Crock Pot Main Dish Recipes

Veggie Curry

Preparation time: 10 minutes
Cooking time: 4 hours
Servings: 4

Ingredients:

- 1 tablespoon ginger, grated
- 14 ounces canned coconut milk
- Cooking spray
- 16 ounces firm tofu, pressed and cubed
- 1 cup veggie stock
- 1/4 cup green curry paste
- 1/2 teaspoon turmeric
- 1 tablespoon coconut sugar
- 1 yellow onion, chopped
- 1 and 1/2 cup red bell pepper, chopped
- A pinch of salt
- 3/4 cup peas
- 1 eggplant, chopped

Directions:

1. Put the coconut milk in your crock pot.
2. Add ginger, stock, curry paste, turmeric, sugar, onion, bell pepper, salt, peas and eggplant pieces, stir, cover and cook on High for 4 hours.
3. Meanwhile, spray a pan with cooking spray and heat up over medium high heat.
4. Add tofu pieces and brown them for a few minutes on each side.
5. Divide tofu into bowls, add slowly cooked curry mix on top and serve.

Enjoy!

Nutrition:

- Calories 200
- Fat 4
- Fiber 6
- Carbs 10
- Protein 9

Classic Black Beans Chili

Preparation time: 10 minutes
Cooking time: 3 hours
Servings: 4

Ingredients:

- 1/2 cup quinoa
- 2 and 1/2 cups veggie stock
- 14 ounces canned tomatoes, chopped
- 15 ounces canned black beans, drained
- 1/4 cup green bell pepper, chopped
- 1/2 cup red bell pepper, chopped
- A pinch of salt and black pepper
- 2 garlic cloves, minced
- 1 carrots, shredded
- 1 small chili pepper, chopped
- 2 teaspoons chili powder
- 1 teaspoon cumin, ground
- A pinch of cayenne pepper
- 1/2 cup corn
- 1 teaspoon oregano, dried

For the vegan sour cream:

- A drizzle of apple cider vinegar
- 4 tablespoons water
- 1/2 cup cashews, soaked overnight and drained
- 1 teaspoon lime juice

Directions:

1. Put the stock in your crock pot.
2. Add quinoa, tomatoes, beans, red and green bell pepper, garlic, carrot, salt, pepper, corn, cumin, cayenne, chili powder, chili pepper and oregano, stir, cover and cook on High for 3 hours.
3. Meanwhile, put the cashews in your blender.
4. Add water, vinegar and lime juice and pulse really well.
5. Divide beans chili into bowls, top with vegan sour cream and serve.
Enjoy!

Nutrition:

- Calories 300
- Fat 4
- Fiber 4
- Carbs 10
- Protein 7

Black Eyed Peas Stew

Preparation time: 10 minutes
Cooking time: 4 hours
Servings: 8

Ingredients:

- 3 celery stalks, chopped
- 2 carrots, sliced
- 1 yellow onion, chopped
- 1 sweet potato, cubed
- 1 green bell pepper, chopped
- 3 cups black-eyed peas, soaked for 8 hours and drained
- 1 cup tomato puree
- 4 cups veggie stock
- A pinch of salt
- Black pepper to the taste
- 1 chipotle chile, minced
- 1 teaspoon ancho chili powder
- 1 teaspoons sage, dried and crumbled
- 2 teaspoons cumin, ground
- Chopped coriander for serving

Directions:

1. Put celery in your crock pot.
2. Add carrots, onion, potato, bell pepper, black-eyed peas, tomato puree, salt, pepper, chili powder, sage, chili, cumin and stock.
3. Stir, cover and cook on High for 4 hours.
4. Stir stew again, divide into bowls and serve with chopped coriander on top.
Enjoy!

Nutrition:

- Calories 200
- Fat 4
- Fiber 7
- Carbs 9
- Protein 16

Light Jackfruit Dish

Preparation time: 10 minutes
Cooking time: 6 hours
Servings: 4

Ingredients:

- 40 ounces green jackfruit in brine, drained
- 1/2 cup agave nectar
- 1/2 cup gluten free tamari sauce
- 1/4 cup soy sauce
- 1 cup white wine
- 2 tablespoons ginger, grated
- 8 garlic cloves, minced
- 1 pear, cored and chopped
- 1 yellow onion, chopped
- 1/2 cup water
- 4 tablespoons sesame oil

Directions:

1. Put jackfruit in your crock pot.
2. Add agave nectar, tamari sauce, soy sauce, wine, ginger, garlic, pear, onion, water and oil.
3. Stir well, cover and cook on Low for 6 hours.
4. Divide jackfruit mix into bowls and serve.

Enjoy!

Nutrition:

- Calories 160
- Fat 4
- Fiber 1
- Carbs 10
- Protein 3

Autumn Veggie Mix

Preparation time: 10 minutes
Cooking time: 4 hours and 30 minutes
Servings: 6

Ingredients:

- 2 sweet potatoes, cubed
- 1 yellow onion, chopped
- 1 small cauliflower head, florets separated
- 14 ounces canned coconut milk
- 2 teaspoons sriracha sauce
- 3 tablespoons coconut aminos
- A pinch of salt
- 1 tablespoon palm sugar
- 3 tablespoons red curry paste
- 1 cup green peas
- 8 ounces white mushrooms, roughly chopped
- 1/2 cup cashews, toasted and chopped
- 1/4 cup cilantro, chopped
- A few basil leaves, chopped for serving
- Brown rice for serving

Directions:

1. Put coconut milk in your crock pot.
2. Add potatoes, onion, cauliflower florets, sriracha sauce, aminos, salt, curry paste and sugar, stir, cover and cook on Low for 4 hours.
3. Add mushrooms, peas, cilantro and basil, stir, cover and cook on Low for 30 minutes more.
4. Divide into bowls and serve with brown rice on the side and toasted cashews on top.

Enjoy!

Nutrition:

- Calories 200
- Fat 3
- Fiber 5
- Carbs 15
- Protein 12

Quinoa and Veggies

Preparation time: 10 minutes
Cooking time: 4 hours
Servings: 4

Ingredients:

- 1 tablespoon olive oil
- 1 and 1/2 cups quinoa
- 3 cups veggie stock
- 1 yellow onion, chopped
- 1 carrot, chopped
- 1 sweet red pepper, chopped
- 1 cup green beans, chopped
- 2 garlic cloves, minced
- 1 teaspoon cilantro, chopped
- A pinch of salt
- Black pepper to the taste

Directions:

1. Put the stock in your crock pot.
2. Add oil, quinoa, onion, carrot, sweet pepper, beans, cloves, salt and pepper, stir, cover and cook on Low for 4 hours.
3. Add cilantro, stir again, divide on plates and serve.

Enjoy!

Nutrition:

- Calories 120
- Fat 2
- Fiber 3
- Carbs 6
- Protein 6

Potato Dish

Preparation time: 10 minutes
Cooking time: 3 hours
Servings: 4

Ingredients:

- 1 and 1/2 pounds potatoes, peeled and roughly chopped
- 1 tablespoon olive oil
- 3 tablespoons water
- 1 small yellow onion, chopped
- 1/2 cup veggie stock cube, crumbled
- 1/2 teaspoon coriander, ground
- 1/2 teaspoon cumin, ground
- 1/2 teaspoon garam masala
- 1/2 teaspoon chili powder
- Black pepper to the taste
- 1/2 pound spinach, roughly torn

Directions:

1. Put the potatoes in your crock pot.
2. Add oil, water, onion, stock cube, coriander, cumin, garam masala, chili powder, black pepper and spinach.
3. Stir, cover and cook on High for 3 hours.
4. Divide into bowls and serve.

Enjoy!

Nutrition:

- Calories 270
- Fat 4
- Fiber 6
- Carbs 8
- Protein 12

Amazing Curry

Preparation time: 10 minutes
Cooking time: 4 hours
Servings: 6

Ingredients:

- 3 cups sweet potatoes, cubed
- 2 cups broccoli florets
- 1 cup water
- 1 cup white onion, chopped
- 28 ounces canned tomatoes, chopped
- 15 ounces canned chickpeas, drained
- 1/4 cup quinoa
- 29 ounces canned coconut milk
- 1 tablespoon garlic, minced
- 1 tablespoon ginger root, grated
- 1 tablespoon turmeric, ground
- 2 teaspoons vegan tamari sauce
- 1 teaspoon chili flakes

Directions:

1. Put the water in your crock pot.
2. Add potatoes, broccoli, onion, tomatoes, chickpeas, quinoa, garlic, ginger, turmeric, chili flakes, tamari sauce and coconut milk.
3. Stir, cover and cook on High for 4 hours.
4. Stir your curry again, divide into bowls and serve.

Enjoy!

Nutrition:

- Calories 400
- Fat 12
- Fiber 10
- Carbs 20
- Protein 10

Indian Lentils

Preparation time: 10 minutes
Cooking time: 3 hours
Servings: 4

Ingredients:

- 1 yellow bell pepper, chopped
- 1 sweet potato, chopped
- 2 and 1/2 cups lentils, already cooked
- 4 garlic cloves, minced
- 1 yellow onion, chopped
- 2 teaspoons cumin, ground
- 15 ounces canned tomato sauce
- 1/2 teaspoon ginger, ground
- A pinch of cayenne pepper
- 1 tablespoons coriander, ground
- 1 teaspoon turmeric, ground
- 2 teaspoons paprika
- 2/3 cup veggie stock
- 1 teaspoon garam masala
- A pinch of sea salt
- Black pepper to the taste
- Juice of 1 lemon

Directions:

1. Put the stock in your crock pot.
2. Add potato, lentils, onion, garlic, cumin, bell pepper, tomato sauce, salt, pepper, ginger, coriander, turmeric, paprika, cayenne, garam masala and lemon juice.
3. Stir, cover and cook on High for 3 hours.
4. Stir your lentils mix again, divide into bowls and serve.

Enjoy!

Nutrition:

- Calories 300
- Fat 6
- Fiber 5
- Carbs 9
- Protein 12

Butternut Squash Soup

Preparation time: 10 minutes
Cooking time: 6 hours
Servings: 8

Ingredients:

- 1 apple, cored, peeled and chopped
- 1/2 pound carrots, chopped
- 1 pound butternut squash, peeled and cubed
- 1 yellow onion, chopped
- A pinch of sea salt
- Black pepper to the taste
- 1 bay leaf
- 3 cups veggie stock
- 14 ounces canned coconut milk
- 1/4 teaspoon sage, dried

Directions:

1. Put the stock in your crock pot.
2. Add apple squash, carrots, onion, salt, pepper and bay leaf.
3. Stir, cover and cook on Low for 6 hours.
4. Transfer to your blender, add coconut milk and sage and pulse really well.
5. Ladle into bowls and serve right away.

Enjoy!

Nutrition:

- Calories 200
- Fat 3
- Fiber 6
- Carbs 8
- Protein 10

Squash Chili

Preparation time: 10 minutes
Cooking time: 6 hours
Servings: 8

Ingredients:

- 2 carrots, chopped
- 1 yellow onion, chopped
- 2 celery stalks, chopped
- 2 green apples, cored, peeled and chopped
- 4 garlic cloves, minced
- 2 cups butternut squash, peeled and cubed
- 6 ounces canned chickpeas, drained
- 6 ounces canned black beans, drained
- 7 ounces canned coconut milk
- 2 teaspoons chili powder
- 1 teaspoon oregano, dried
- 1 tablespoon cumin, ground
- 2 cups veggie stock
- 2 tablespoons tomato paste
- Salt and black pepper to the taste
- 1 tablespoon cilantro, chopped

Directions:

1. In your crock pot, mix carrots with onion, celery, apples, garlic, squash, chickpeas, black beans, coconut milk, chili powder, oregano, cumin, stock, tomato paste, salt and pepper, stir, cover and cook on High for 6 hours.
2. Add cilantro, stir, divide into bowls and serve.

Enjoy!

Nutrition:

- Calories 312
- Fat 6
- Fiber 8
- Carbs 12
- Protein 6

Pumpkin Chili

Preparation time: 10 minutes
Cooking time: 8 hours
Servings: 6

Ingredients:

- 1 cup pumpkin, pureed
- 45 ounces canned black beans, drained
- 30 ounces canned tomatoes, chopped
- 1 yellow bell pepper, chopped
- 1 yellow onion, chopped
- 1/4 teaspoon nutmeg, ground
- 1 teaspoon cinnamon powder
- 1 tablespoon chili powder
- 1 teaspoon cumin, ground
- 1/8 teaspoon cloves, ground
- A pinch of sea salt
- Black pepper to the taste

Directions:

1. Put pumpkin puree in your crock pot.
2. Add black beans, tomatoes, onion, bell pepper, cumin, nutmeg, cinnamon, chili powder, cloves, salt and pepper, stir, cover and cook on Low for 8 hours.
3. Stir your chili again, divide into bowls and serve.

Enjoy!

Nutrition:

- Calories 250
- Fat 5
- Fiber 9
- Carbs 12
- Protein 8

Beans Soup

Preparation time: 10 minutes
Cooking time: 7 hours
Servings: 4

Ingredients:

- 1 pound navy beans
- 1 yellow onion, chopped
- 4 garlic cloves, crushed
- 2 quarts veggie stock
- A pinch of sea salt
- Black pepper to the taste
- 2 potatoes, peeled and cubed
- 2 teaspoons dill, dried
- 1 cup sun-dried tomatoes, chopped
- 1 pound carrots, sliced
- 4 tablespoons parsley, minced

Directions:

1. Put the stock in your crock pot.
2. Add beans, onion, garlic, potatoes, tomatoes, carrots, dill, salt and pepper, stir, cover and cook on Low for 7 hours.
3. Stir your soup, add parsley, divide into bowls and serve.

Enjoy!

Nutrition:

- Calories 250
- Fat 4
- Fiber 3
- Carbs 9
- Protein 10

Tofu Dish

Preparation time: 10 minutes
Cooking time: 3 hours
Servings: 6

Ingredients:

- 1 big tofu package, cubed
- 1 tablespoon sesame oil
- 1/4 cup pineapple, cubed
- 1 tablespoon olive oil
- 2 garlic cloves, minced
- 1 tablespoons brown rice vinegar
- 2 teaspoon ginger, grated
- 1/4 cup soy sauce
- 5 big zucchinis, cubed
- 1/4 cup sesame seeds

Directions:

1. In your food processor, mix sesame oil with pineapple, olive oil, garlic, ginger, soy sauce and vinegar and whisk well.
2. Add this to your crock pot and mix with tofu cubes.
3. Cover and cook on High for 2 hours and 45 minutes.
4. Add sesame seeds and zucchinis, stir gently, cover and cook on High for 15 minutes.
5. Divide between plates and serve.
Enjoy!

Nutrition:

- Calories 200
- Fat 3
- Fiber 4
- Carbs 9
- Protein 10

Sweet Potatoes and Lentils

Preparation time: 10 minutes
Cooking time: 4 hours and 30 minutes
Servings: 6

Ingredients:

- 6 cups sweet potatoes, peeled and cubed
- 2 teaspoons coriander, ground
- 2 teaspoons chili powder
- 1 yellow onion, chopped
- 3 cups veggie stock
- 4 garlic cloves, minced
- A pinch of sea salt and black pepper
- 10 ounces canned coconut milk
- 1 cup water
- 1 and 1/2 cups red lentils

Directions:

1. Put sweet potatoes in your crock pot.
2. Add coriander, chili powder, onion, stock, garlic, salt and pepper, stir, cover and cook on High for 3 hours.
3. Add lentils, stir, cover and cook for 1 hour and 30 minutes.
4. Add water and coconut milk, stir well, divide into bowls and serve right away.

Enjoy!

Nutrition:

- Calories 300
- Fat 10
- Fiber 8
- Carbs 16
- Protein 10

Chinese Tofu and Veggies

Preparation time: 10 minutes
Cooking time: 4 hours
Servings: 4

Ingredients:

- 14 ounces extra firm tofu, pressed and cut into medium triangles
- Cooking spray
- 2 teaspoons ginger, grated
- 1 yellow onion, chopped
- 3 garlic cloves, minced
- 8 ounces tomato sauce
- 1/4 cup hoisin sauce
- 1/4 teaspoon coconut aminos
- 2 tablespoons rice wine vinegar
- 1 tablespoon soy sauce
- 1 tablespoon spicy mustard
- 1/4 teaspoon red pepper, crushed
- 2 teaspoons molasses
- 2 tablespoons water
- A pinch of black pepper
- 3 broccoli stalks
- 1 green bell pepper, cut into squares
- 2 zucchinis, cubed

Directions:

1. Heat up a pan over medium high heat, add tofu pieces, brown them for a few minutes and transfer to your crock pot.
2. Heat up the pan again over medium high heat, add ginger, onion, garlic and tomato sauce, stir, sauté for a few minutes and transfer to your crock pot as well.
3. Add hoisin sauce, aminos, vinegar, soy sauce, mustard, red pepper, molasses, water and black pepper, stir gently, cover and cook on High for 3 hours.
4. Add zucchinis, bell pepper and broccoli, cover and cook on High for 1 more hour.
5. Divide between plates and serve right away.

Enjoy!

Nutrition:

- Calories 300
- Fat 4
- Fiber 8
- Carbs 14
- Protein 13

Eggplant Salad

Preparation time: 10 minutes
Cooking time: 8 hours
Servings: 4

Ingredients:

- 1 big eggplant, cut into quarters and then sliced
- 25 ounces canned plum tomatoes
- 2 red bell peppers, chopped
- 1 red onion, sliced
- 2 teaspoons cumin, ground
- A pinch of sea salt
- Black pepper to the taste
- 1 teaspoon smoked paprika
- Juice of 1 lemon

Directions:

1. In your crock pot, mix eggplant pieces with tomatoes, bell peppers, onion, cumin, salt, pepper, paprika and lemon juice, stir, cover and cook on Low for 8 hours.
2. Stir again, divide into bowls and serve cold.

Enjoy!

Nutrition:

- Calories 143
- Fat 2
- Fiber 3
- Carbs 7
- Protein 8

Black Beans Soup

Preparation time: 10 minutes
Cooking time: 6 hours
Servings: 6

Ingredients:

- 4 cups veggie stock
- 1 pound black beans, soaked overnight and drained
- 1 yellow onion, chopped
- 2 jalapenos, chopped
- 1 red bell pepper, chopped
- 1 cup tomatoes, chopped
- 4 garlic cloves, minced
- 1 tablespoon chili powder
- Black pepper to the taste
- 2 teaspoons cumin, ground
- A pinch of sea salt
- 1/2 teaspoon cayenne pepper
- 1 avocado, pitted, peeled and chopped
- 1/2 teaspoon sweet paprika

Directions:

1. Put the stock in your crock pot.
2. Add beans, onion, jalapenos, bell pepper, tomatoes, garlic, chili powder, black pepper, salt, cumin, cayenne and paprika.
3. Stir, cover and cook on Low for 6 hours.
4. Blend soup using an immersion blender, ladle into bowls and serve with chopped avocado on top.

Enjoy!

Nutrition:

- Calories 200
- Fat 2
- Fiber 3
- Carbs 7
- Protein 17

Chickpeas Soup

Preparation time: 10 minutes
Cooking time: 4 hours
Servings: 6

Ingredients:

- 30 ounces canned chickpeas, drained
- 2 tablespoons mild curry powder
- 1 cup lentils, dry
- 1 sweet potato, cubed
- 15 ounces canned coconut milk
- 1 teaspoon ginger powder
- 1 teaspoon turmeric, ground
- A pinch of salt
- 6 cups veggie stock
- Black pepper to the taste

Directions:

1. Put chickpeas in your crock pot.
2. Add lentils, sweet potato cubes, curry powder, ginger, turmeric, salt, pepper and stock.
3. Stir and then mix with coconut milk.
4. Stir again, cover and cook on High for 4 hours.
5. Ladle chickpeas soup into bowls and serve.

Enjoy!

Nutrition:

- Calories 210
- Fat 4
- Fiber 6
- Carbs 9
- Protein 12

Vegan Chickpeas Winter Mix

Preparation time: 10 minutes
Cooking time: 4 hours and 10 minutes
Servings: 6

Ingredients:

- 1 yellow onion, chopped
- 1 tablespoon ginger, grated
- 1 tablespoon olive oil
- 4 garlic cloves, minced
- A pinch of salt and black pepper
- 2 red Thai chilies, chopped
- 1/2 teaspoon turmeric powder
- 2 tablespoons garam masala
- 4 ounces tomato paste
- 2 cups veggie stock
- 6 ounces canned chickpeas, drained
- 2 tablespoons cilantro, chopped

Directions:

1. Heat up a pan with the oil over medium high heat, add ginger and onions, stir and cook for 4-5 minutes.
2. Add garlic, salt, pepper, Thai chilies, garam masala and turmeric, stir, cook for 2 minutes more and transfer everything to your crock pot.
3. Add stock, chickpeas and tomato paste, stir, cover and cook on Low for 4 hours.
4. Add cilantro, stir, divide into bowls and serve.

Enjoy!

Nutrition:

- Calories 211
- Fat 7
- Fiber 4
- Carbs 9
- Protein 7

Chapter 7: Vegan Crock Pot Dessert Recipes

Peanut Butter Cake

Preparation time: 10 minutes
Cooking time: 2 hours and 30 minutes
Servings: 6

Ingredients:

- 1 cup almond flour
- 1/2 cup coconut sugar
- 3/4 cup coconut sugar
- 3 tablespoons cocoa powder
- 1/4 cup cocoa powder
- 1 and 1/2 teaspoons baking powder
- 2 tablespoons vegan margarine, melted
- 1/2 cup soy milk
- 1 teaspoon vanilla extract
- 1/2 cup peanut butter
- 2 cups hot water
- Cooking spray

Directions:

1. In a bowl, mix flour with 1/2 cup sugar, baking powder and 3 tablespoons cocoa powder and stir well.
2. Add margarine, soy milk and vanilla and stir well.
3. Grease your crock pot with cooking spray and pour the cake mix in it.
4. In another bowl, mix 1/4 cup cocoa powder with 3/4 cup sugar and stir.
5. In a second bowl, mix peanut butter with hot water and whisk really well.
6. Combine cocoa powder mix with peanut butter one and stir everything.
7. Pour this over your cake batter, cover and cook on High for 2 hours and 30 minutes.
8. Leave the cake to cool down a bit, slice and serve.

Enjoy!

Nutrition:

- Calories 220
- Fat 3
- Fiber 4
- Carbs 6
- Protein 10

Pear Delight

Preparation time: 10 minutes
Cooking time: 4 hours
Servings: 12

Ingredients:

- 3 pears, cored, peeled and chopped
- 1/2 cup raisins
- 2 cups dried fruits, mixed
- 1/4 cup coconut sugar
- 1 tablespoon vinegar
- 1 teaspoon lemon zest, grated
- 1 teaspoon ginger powder
- A pinch of cinnamon powder

Directions:

1. Put the pears in your crock pot.
2. Add raisins, fruits, sugar, vinegar, lemon zest, ginger powder and cinnamon, stir, cover and cook on Low for 4 hours.
3. Divide into small jars and serve whenever!

Enjoy!

Nutrition:

- Calories 140
- Fat 3
- Fiber 4
- Carbs 6
- Protein 6

Apple Crisp

Preparation time: 10 minutes
Cooking time: 3 hours
Servings: 6

Ingredients:

- 6 apples, cored, peeled and sliced
- 1 and 1/2 cups almond flour
- Cooking spray
- 1 cup palm sugar
- 1/2 teaspoon nutmeg, ground
- 1 tablespoon cinnamon powder
- 1/4 teaspoon ginger powder
- 3/4 cup coconut butter, melted

Directions:

1. Grease your crock pot with cooking spray and arrange apple slices on it.
2. In a bowl, mix flour with palm sugar, ginger, cinnamon, nutmeg and coconut butter and stir using your hands.
3. Spread this mix over your apple slices, cover crock pot and cook on High for 3 hours.
4. Divide into dessert bowls and serve.

Enjoy!

Nutrition:

- Calories 160
- Fat 5
- Fiber 5
- Carbs 12
- Protein 6

Stewed Rhubarb

Preparation time: 10 minutes
Cooking time: 7 hours
Servings: 4

Ingredients:

- 5 cups rhubarb, chopped
- 2 tablespoons coconut butter
- 1/3 cup water
- 2/3 cup coconut sugar
- 1 teaspoon vanilla extract

Directions:

1. Put rhubarb in your crock pot.
2. Add water and sugar, stir gently, cover and cook on Low for 7 hours.
3. Add coconut butter and vanilla extract, stir and keep in the fridge until it's cold.
Enjoy!

Nutrition:

- Calories 120
- Fat 2
- Fiber 3
- Carbs 6
- Protein 1

Wonderful Plum Butter

Preparation time: 10 minutes
Cooking time: 10 hours
Servings: 10

Ingredients:

- 4 pounds plums, pitted and halved
- 1 cup water
- 1 teaspoon cinnamon, ground
- 1/2 teaspoon cardamom, ground
- 1 cup palm sugar

Directions:

1. Put plums and water in your crock pot.
2. Cover and cook on Low for 1 hour.
3. Stir, add cinnamon, sugar and cardamom, stir, cover and cook on Low for 9 more hours.
4. Stir really well, divide into jars and serve.

Enjoy!

Nutrition:

- Calories 100
- Fat 2
- Fiber 1
- Carbs 3
- Protein 6

Sweet Peanut Butter Cake

Preparation time: 10 minutes
Cooking time: 2 hours and 30 minutes
Servings: 8

Ingredients:

- 1 cup coconut sugar
- 1 cup flour
- 3 tablespoons cocoa powder + 1/2 cup
- 1 and 1/2 teaspoons baking powder
- 1/2 cup almond milk
- 2 tablespoons coconut oil
- 2 cups hot water
- 1 teaspoon vanilla extract
- 1/2 cup peanut butter
- Cooking spray

Directions:

1. In a bowl, mix half of the coconut sugar with 3 tablespoons cocoa, flour and baking powder and stir well.
2. Add coconut oil, vanilla and milk, stir well and pour into your crock pot greased with cooking spray.
3. In another bowl, mix the rest of the sugar with the rest of the cocoa, peanut butter and hot water, stir well and pour over the batter in the crock pot.
4. Cover pot, cook on High for 2 hours and 30 minutes, slice cake and serve.

Enjoy!

Nutrition:

- Calories 242
- Fat 4
- Fiber 7
- Carbs 8
- Protein 4

Strawberry Jam

Preparation time: 10 minutes
Cooking time: 3 hours
Servings: 12

Ingredients:

- 2 tablespoons lemon juice
- 4 pints strawberries
- 4 cups coconut sugar

Directions:

1. Put strawberries in your crock pot.
2. Add lemon juice and stir gently.
3. Add sugar, stir again, cover and cook on Low for 1 hour.
4. Stir and cook on Low for 1 more hour.
5. Stir again and cook for 1 last hour.
6. Divide into jars and serve whenever you like.

Enjoy!

Nutrition:

- Calories 30
- Fat 0
- Fiber 1
- Carbs 6
- Protein 1

Apple Mix

Preparation time: 10 minutes
Cooking time: 4 hours
Servings: 6

Ingredients:

- 6 apples, cored, peeled and sliced
- 1 and 1/2 cups almond flour
- Cooking spray
- 1 cup coconut sugar
- 1 tablespoon cinnamon powder
- 3/4 cup cashew butter, melted

Directions:

1. Add apple slices to your crock pot after you've greased it with cooking spray
2. Add flour, sugar, cinnamon and coconut butter, stir gently, cover, cook on High for 4 hours, divide into bowls and serve cold.

Enjoy!

Nutrition:

- Calories 200
- Fat 5
- Fiber 5
- Carbs 8
- Protein 4

Strawberries Jan

Preparation time: 10 minutes
Cooking time: 4 hours
Servings: 10

Ingredients:

- 32 ounces strawberries, chopped
- 2 pounds coconut sugar
- Zest of 1 lemon, grated
- 4 ounces raisins
- 3 ounces water

Directions:

1. In your crock pot, mix strawberries with coconut sugar, lemon zest, raisins and water, stir, cover and cook on High for 4 hours.
2. Divide into small jars and serve cold.

Enjoy!

Nutrition:

- Calories 100
- Fat 3
- Fiber 2
- Carbs 2
- Protein 1

Strawberry Cobbler

Preparation time: 10 minutes
Cooking time: 2 hours
Servings: 4

Ingredients:

- 2 teaspoons baking powder
- 1 and 1/4 cups coconut sugar
- 2 and 1/2 cups almond flour
- 1/2 teaspoon cinnamon powder
- 2 tablespoons flax seed meal mixed with 1 tablespoon water
- 1/2 cup almond milk
- 4 tablespoons canola oil
- 6 cups strawberries, chopped
- 1/4 cup rolled oats
- 1/4 cup basil, chopped
- Cooking spray

Directions:

1. In a bowl, mix 2 cups flour with 1/4 cup sugar, baking powder, cinnamon, milk, oil and flax seed meal and stir really well.
2. In another bowl, mix the rest of the flour with the rest of the sugar, basil and strawberries and toss well.
3. Pour the batter into your crock pot after you've sprayed with cooking spray and spread well.
4. Add strawberries mix on top, sprinkle rolled oats, cover and cook on High for 2 hours.
5. Leave cobbler to cool down a bit and serve.

Enjoy!

Nutrition:

- Calories 130
- Fat 4
- Fiber 3
- Carbs 8
- Protein 7

Amazing Hot Fruits

Preparation time: 10 minutes
Cooking time: 4 hours
Servings: 10

Ingredients:

- 20 ounces canned pineapple chunks, drained
- 21 ounces canned cherries, drained
- 15 ounces canned apricots, halved and drained
- 15 ounces canned peach slices, drained
- 25 ounces vegan applesauce
- 15 ounces canned mandarin oranges, drained
- 1/4 cup coconut sugar
- 1 teaspoon cinnamon powder

Directions:

1. Put pineapple pieces in your crock pot.
2. Add cherries, apricots, peaches, applesauce, oranges, cinnamon and sugar.
3. Stir gently, cover and cook on Low for 4 hours.
4. Divide into bowls and serve warm.

Enjoy!

Nutrition:

- Calories 200
- Fat 3
- Fiber 2
- Carbs 10
- Protein 2

Peach Cobbler

Preparation time: 10 minutes
Cooking time: 4 hours
Servings: 4

Ingredients:

- 4 cups peaches, peeled and sliced
- 1/4 cup coconut sugar
- 1/2 teaspoon cinnamon powder
- 1 and 1/2 cups vegan sweet crackers, crushed
- 1/4 cup stevia
- 1/4 teaspoon nutmeg, ground
- 1/2 cup almond milk
- 1 teaspoon vanilla extract
- Cooking spray

Directions:

1. In a bowl, mix peaches with coconut sugar and cinnamon and stir.
2. In a separate bowl, mix crackers with stevia, nutmeg, almond milk and vanilla extract and stir.
3. Spray your crock pot with cooking spray and spread peaches on the bottom.
4. Add crackers mix, spread, cover and cook on Low for 4 hours.
5. Divide cobbler between plates and serve.

Enjoy!

Nutrition:

- Calories 212
- Fat 4
- Fiber 4
- Carbs 7
- Protein 3

Orange Cake

Preparation time: 10 minutes
Cooking time: 5 hours
Servings: 4

Ingredients:

- Cooking spray
- 1 teaspoon baking powder
- 1 cup almond flour
- 1 cup coconut sugar
- 1/2 teaspoon cinnamon powder
- 3 tablespoons coconut oil, melted
- 1/2 cup almond milk
- 1/2 pecans, chopped
- 3/4 cup water
- 1/2 cup raisins
- 1/2 cup orange peel, grated
- 3/4 cup orange juice

Directions:

1. In a bowl, mix flour with half of the sugar, baking powder, cinnamon, 2 tablespoons oil, milk, pecans and raisins, stir and pour this in your crock pot after you've sprayed it with cooking spray.
2. Heat up a small pan over medium heat, add water, orange juice, orange peel, the rest of the oil and the rest of the sugar, stir, bring to a boil, pour over the mix in the crock pot, cover and cook on Low for 5 hours.
3. Divide into dessert bowls and serve cold.

Enjoy!

Nutrition:

- Calories 182
- Fat 3
- Fiber 1
- Carbs 4
- Protein 3

Peach Cake

Preparation time: 10 minutes
Cooking time: 2 hours and 30 minutes
Servings: 8

Ingredients:

- 10 tablespoons coconut butter, melted
- 45 ounces canned peaches, drained
- 1 and 2/3 cup palm sugar
- 1 teaspoon cinnamon powder
- 1/2 teaspoon nutmeg
- 1/2 teaspoon almond extract
- 2 teaspoons baking powder
- 2 tablespoons flaxseed meal mixed with 1 tablespoon water
- 2 cups almond flour
- 1 cup coconut milk

Directions:

1. Drizzle half of the butter on the bottom of your crock pot.
2. In a bowl mix nutmeg with 2/3 cup sugar and cinnamon and stir well.
3. Spread this over the butter in your crock pot.
4. Arrange peaches next and spread them evenly in the pot.
5. In a bowl, mix the rest of the butter with the rest of the sugar, coconut milk, almond extract and flaxseed meal and stir well.
6. In another bowl, mix flour with baking powder and stir.
7. Combine butter and sugar mix with the flour and stir well.
8. Pour this over the peaches, cover and cook on High for 2 hours and 3 o minutes.
9. Leave the cake to cool down a bit and turn it upside down on a platter.
10. Serve cold.
Enjoy!

Nutrition:

- Calories 200
- Fat 4
- Fiber 5
- Carbs 7
- Protein 8

Pears And Orange Sauce

Preparation time: 10 minutes
Cooking time: 4 hours
Servings: 4

Ingredients:

- 4 pears, peeled and cored
- 2 cups orange juice
- 1/4 cup maple syrup
- 2 teaspoons cinnamon powder
- 1 tablespoon ginger, grated

Directions:

1. In your crock pot, mix pears with orange juice, maple syrup, cinnamon and ginger, cover and cook on Low for 4 hours.
2. Divide pears and orange sauce between plates and serve warm.

Enjoy!

Nutrition:

- Calories 140
- Fat 1
- Fiber 2
- Carbs 3
- Protein 4

Easy Almond Pudding

Preparation time: 10 minutes
Cooking time: 2 hours and 30 minutes
Servings: 6

Ingredients:

- 1 mandarin, sliced
- Juice from 2 mandarins
- 2 tablespoons coconut sugar
- 4 ounces coconut butter, soft
- 2 tablespoons flax seed meal mixed with 1 tablespoon water
- 3/4 cup coconut sugar
- 3/4 cup almond flour
- 1 teaspoon baking powder
- 3/4 cup almonds, ground Cooking spray

Directions:

1. Grease a loaf pan cooking spray and sprinkle 2 tablespoons sugar on the bottom.
2. Arrange sliced Mandarin over the sugar and leave loaf pan aside for now.
3. In a bowl, mix butter with 3/4 cup sugar and flax seed meal mixed with water and stir really well.
4. Add almonds, flour, baking powder and the mandarin juice and stir again.
5. Spread this over mandarin slices, arrange pan in your crock pot, cover and cook on High for 2 hours and 30 minutes.
6. Uncover, leave aside for a few minutes, transfer to a platter, slice and serve.

Enjoy!

Nutrition:

- Calories 200
- Fat 4
- Fiber 2
- Carbs 5
- Protein 6

Spicy Pears

Preparation time: 10 minutes
Cooking time: 4 hours
Servings: 2

Ingredients:

- 2 cups orange juice
- 4 pears, peeled and cored
- 5 cardamom pods
- 1/4 cup maple syrup
- 1 cinnamon stick
- 1 small ginger piece, grated

Directions:

1. Place pears in your crock pot.
2. Add cardamom, orange juice, maple syrup, cinnamon and ginger, cover and cook on Low for 4 hours.
3. Divide pears between plates and serve.

Enjoy!

Nutrition:

- Calories 130
- Fat 2
- Fiber 3
- Carbs 6
- Protein 4

Fruit Compote

Preparation time: 10 minutes
Cooking time: 4 hours
Servings: 6

Ingredients:

- 1-quart water
- 1 cup coconut sugar
- 1 pound mixed apples, pears and cranberries, dried
- 5-star anise
- 2 cinnamon sticks
- Zest from 1 orange, grated
- A pinch cloves, ground
- Zest from 1 lemon, grated

Directions:

1. Put the water and the sugar in your crock pot and stir well.
2. Add dried fruits, star anise, cinnamon, orange and lemon zest and cloves.
3. Stir, cover and cook on High for 4 hours.
4. Serve your compote warm in small dessert cups.

Enjoy!

Nutrition:

- Calories 110
- Fat 0
- Fiber 2
- Carbs 3
- Protein 5

Pears And Dried Fruits Bowls

Preparation time: 10 minutes
Cooking time: 4 hours
Servings: 12

Ingredients:

- 3 pears, cored and chopped
- 1/2 cup raisins
- 2 cups dried fruits
- 1 teaspoon ginger powder
- 1/4 cup coconut sugar
- 1 teaspoon lemon zest, grated

Directions:

1. In your crock pot, mix pears with raisins, dried fruits, ginger, sugar and lemon zest, stir, cover, cook on Low for 4 hours, divide into bowls and serve cold.

Enjoy!

Nutrition:

- Calories 140
- Fat 3
- Fiber 4
- Carbs 6
- Protein 6

Stewed Plums

Preparation time: 10 minutes
Cooking time: 3 hours
Servings: 6

Ingredients:

- 14 plums, halved and pitted
- 1 and 1/4 cups coconut sugar
- 1 teaspoon cinnamon, ground
- 1/4 cup water
- 2 tablespoons vegan cornstarch

Directions:

2. Put plums in your crock pot.
3. Add sugar, cinnamon, water and cornstarch, stir, cover and cook on Low for 3 hours.
4. Divide into small jars, seal them and serve as a dessert.

Enjoy!

Nutrition:

- Calories 100
- Fat 2
- Fiber 1
- Carbs 4
- Protein 8

Conclusion

Whether you are a dedicated vegan, a moderate vegetarian, or just a weekend herbivore, The Vegan Crock Pot Cookbook is your simple source for recipes that fit into your busy life. With hands-off recipes, it proves you can spend minutes in the kitchen and still have a delicious end result.

The Vegan Crock Pot Cookbook is filled with simple dishes that involve no pre-cooking and that rarely exceed 10 minutes of prep time. Simply load your crock pot with raw ingredients, go about your day, and return to a ready-to-serve meal.

Get a copy of Vegan Crock Pot Cookbook and see how it can help you become healthier and happier!

CPSIA information can be obtained
at www.ICGtesting.com
Printed in the USA
BVHW010303131221
623904BV00003B/279